The Cornish Consonantal System

Implications for the Revival

by

Nicholas Williams
MA PhD DipCeltStud FLS ITIA
Emeritus Professor in Celtic Languages
University College, Dublin

evertype
2016

Published by / *Dyllys gans* Evertype, 72 Woodgrove, Portlaoise, R32 ENP6, Ireland / *Wordhen*.
www.evertype.com.

First edition 2016.
Kensa dyllans 2016.

Editor / *Penscrefer*: Michael Everson.

Y kefyr covath rolyans rag an lyver-ma dhyworth an Lyverva Vretennek.
A catalogue record for this book is available from dhe British Library.

ISBN-10 1-78201-185-4
ISBN-13 978-1-78201-185-9

Typeset in Palatino by Michael Everson.
Olsettys yn Palatino gans Michael Everson.

Cover / *Cudhlen*: Michael Everson

Printed by / *Pryntys gans* LightningSource.

CONTENTS

FOREWORD

Because we have no native speakers of Cornish, there is always the danger that as revivalists we will shape the revived language according to certain preconceptions. This was certainly true of Jenner and Nance. Revivalists should perhaps be more careful to study thoroughly the remains of the traditional language, and base their speech on what is found in the texts rather than on either of the other Brythonic languages. This is as true for matters of orthography and phonology as it is for the lexicon.

In the following pages certain aspects of the consonantal system of Cornish are analysed as they appear in the surviving texts. Some of the views put forward will not have been seen in print before. Thereafter some suggestions have been made by which the Standard Written Form might be emended to render it less unsatisfactory.

Nicholas Williams
Dublin, 2016

ABBREVIATIONS AND REFERENCES

AB = Edward Lhuyd, *Archæologia Britannica* (London 1707 [reprinted Shannon 1971])

ACB = William Pryce, *Archæologia Cornu-Britannica* (Sherborne 1790 [reprinted by The Scholar Press, Menston, Yorkshire 1972])

ADLD = William Rowe, *An Deeg Lavarow a Deew* [The Ten Commandments]. http://www.moderncornish.net/late-texts/Rowe-William-tencommandments.html

An Awayl herwyth Sen Jowan = John Page (translator), *The Gospel according to St John in Cornish* (Dyllansow Truran 1984)

BF = O. J. Padel, *The Cornish Writings of the Boson Family* (Redruth 1975)

Bilbao MS = Henry Jenner, 'The Cornish Manuscript in the provincial library at Bilbao, Spain', *Journal of the Royal Institution of Cornwall* 21 (192-25): 421-37

BK = Graham Thomas, Nicholas Williams (editors), *Bewnans Ke: The Life of St Kea: A critical edition with translation*. University of Exeter Press in association with The National Library of Wales (2007). ISBN 978-0-85989-800-3

BM = Whitley Stokes (ed.), *Beunans Meriasek: the life of St Meriasek, Bishop and confessor, a Cornish drama* (London: Trübner and Co. 1872)

Bodinar = *William Bodinar's letter*, text from LAM: 244. See also http://www.moderncornish.net/late-texts/Bodinar-William-lettertobarrington.html

Carew = F. E. Halliday (ed.), *Richard Carew of Antony: the survey of Cornwall* (London 1953)

CF = *The Charter Fragment*, text from Harry Woodhouse (editor), *The Cornish Passion Poem in facsimile*. Gorseth Kernow (2002). ISBN 1-903668-02-6, pp. 102-03

CPNE = O. J. Padel, *Cornish Place-name Elements* (Nottingham 1985)

CPT = William C. Borlase, 'A Collection of hitherto unpublished Proverbs and Rhymes in the Ancient Cornish Language; from the Manuscript of Dr. Borlase,' *Journal of the Royal Institution of Cornwall* 2/1 (1866), pp. 7-14

Crankan = John Davey, *Crankan Rhyme* c. 1890. http://home.btconnect.com/htm_cornwall/traditional%20texts/davey_j_jnr_crankan.html

CT3 = Nicholas Williams, *Cornish Today: an examination of the revived language*, third edition (Cathair na Mart: Evertype 2006, ISBN 978-1-904808-07-7)

CW = Whitley Stokes (editor), Gwreans an Bys: The Creation of the World, A Cornish Mystery. (London 1864 [reprinted. Kessinger Publishing. ISBN 0-7661-8009-3]

ÉCII = Joseph Loth, 'Etudes Corniques ii, textes inédits en cornique moderne', *Revue Celtique* 23 (1902), 173-200

GG = Nicholas Williams, *Geryow Gwir: The Lexicon of Revived Cornish*. Second edition. (Cathair na Mart 2014). ISBN 978-1-78201-068-5

Handbook = Henry Jenner, *A Handbook of the Cornish Language, chiefly in its latest stages with some account of its history and literature*. (London 1904)

HPB = Kenneth Hurlstone Jackson, *A Historical Phonology of Breton* (Dublin 1967)

Jago = Fred W. P. Jago, *The Ancient Language, and the Dialect of Cornwall, with an Enlarged Glossary of Cornish Provincial Words* (London 1882)

KG1 = ?John Keigwin, *Genesis* chapter 1, British Library Add MS 28554, ff 117r-119v. http://www.bibelkernewek.com/jkg1.htm

ABBREVIATIONS AND REFERENCES

LAM = Alan M. Kent and Tim Saunders (editors), *Looking at the Mermaid: a reader in Cornish literature 900-1900* (London 2000) ISBN 1-903427-01-0

Loth 1900 = 'Cornique Moderne', in W. Stokes and K. Meyer, *Archiv für Celtische Lexicographie, I Band* (Halle 1900), 224-29. Editions of Cornish dialogue from Borde's Introduction to Knowledge and of William Bodener's letter.

Malone = Malone, Kemp, 'When Did Middle English Begin?, *Language,* vol. 6, no. 4, Language Monograph no. 7: Curme Volume of Linguistic Studies (Dec. 1930), 110-17

MB = Middle Breton

MC = Middle Cornish

ME = Middle English

Mills 1999 = Jon Mills, "Reconstructive Phonology and Contrastive Lexicography: Problems with the Gerlyver Kernewek Kemmyn", in *Cornish Studies*. Second series: Seven. Exeter: University of Exeter Press. Pp. 193-218. ISBN 0-85989-644-7

Norris 1859 = Edwin Norris, *The Ancient Cornish Drama* i-ii (London [reprinted New York/London, Benjamin Blom 1968])

OC = Old Cornish

OCV = Eugene Van Tassel Graves, *The Old Cornish Vocabulary*, Columbia University, PhD 1962 Language and Literature, linguistics. University Microfilms, Inc., Ann Arbor, Michigan

OM = 'Origo Mundi' in Norris, *The Ancient Cornish Drama* i-ii (London 1859 [reprinted New York 1968]) i: 1-219

PA = *Pascon agan Arluth* "The Passion of our Lord", text from Harry Woodhouse, *The Cornish Passion Poem in facsimile* (Penryn 2002) ISBN 1-903668-02-6

PC = 'Passio Christi Nostri Jhesu Christi' in Norris, *The Ancient Cornish Drama* i-ii (London 1859 [reprinted New York 1968])i: 221-479

PS = the Prosodic Shift

Price (1992) = Glanville Price, 'Cornish Language and Literature', in Glanville Price (editor), *The Celtic Connection*: Princess Grace Irish Library: 6. Gerrards Cross (1992). ISBN 0-86140-248-0

RC = *Revue Celtique*

RD = 'Resurrexio Domini Nostri Jhesu Christi' in Norris (1859) in Norris, *The Ancient Comish Drama* i-ii (London 1859 [reprinted New York 1968]) ii: 1-199

RComm. = William Rowe, Ten Commandments in Cornish: An Deeg Lavarow Deew. http://www.moderncornish.net/late-texts/Rowe-William-tencommandments.html

RCEV = Andre Hawke, 'A Rediscovered Cornish-English Vocabulary', *Cornish Studies* (Second Series) *Nine* (Exeter 2001), 83-104

SA = *Sacrament an Alter* "Sacrament of the Altar" text quoted from an unpublished edition by D.H. Frost, *Sacrament an Alter: Part II* (St David's College 2003)

SDMC = Richard R. M. Gendall, *A Student's Dictionary of Modern Cornish* (Menheniot 1993)

SWF = Single Written Form (of revived Cornish)

Symonds = Richard Symonds, Civil War Diary. http://home.btconnect.com/htm_cornwall/traditional%20texts/symonds_1644.html

TH = John Tregear, *Homelyes xiii in Cornysche* (British Library Additional Manuscript 46, 397) [text from a cyclostyled text published by Christopher Bice (s.l.) 1969). See also: https://wikisource.org/wiki/Homelyes_XIII_in_Cornysche

Wakelin = Martyn F. Wakelin, *Language and history in Cornwall* (Leicester: Leicester University Press 1975)

Williams (2007) = 'A review of *The New Testament* in Kernowek Kemmyn' in Michael Everson, et al., *Form and Content in Revived Cornish*. Cathair na Mart: Evertype. ISBN 978-1-904808-10-7.

CHAPTER 1
Preliminary considerations

1.1 Writing in 1897 Joseph Loth makes the following statement:

> Les regrets que peut nous causer l'extinction du cornique sont, en partie, atténués par le fait que les deux langues brittoniques vivantes en sont très voisines, le breton surtout qui forme avec le cornique un groupe si intime qu'on peut les considérer comme deux dialectes voisins d'une même langue. Le cornique moyen était incontestablement moins éloigné du breton-armoricain pris dans son ensemble que le breton de Quiberon ne l'est actuellement de celui de Saint-Pol-de-Léon.
>
> [Our regrets at the death of Cornish are in some part alleviated by the fact that the two living Brythonic languages are very close to it, Breton in particular forming with Cornish such a close linguistic group that we can consider them as two related dialects of the same language. Middle Cornish was without doubt closer to Breton as a whole than the modern Breton dialect of Quiberon to that of St-Pol-de-Léon] (RC 18: 401-02).

Loth knew Cornish well and Breton very well. It is remarkable, therefore, that he should have made such a demonstrably untrue claim about the two languages. Middle Cornish and Middle Breton were not simply dialects of the same language, as will be shown below. Loth's claim is particularly unfortunate in that more recent commentators have taken it at face value and have attempted to fit revived Cornish into the straitjacket of Breton phonology and orthography.

Although Middle Breton and Middle Cornish are close, one would not *a priori* assume that they were nothing more than two dialects of the same language. After all Cornish is a variety of South-West Brythonic, still spoken in its place of origin, but developing in the ambit of Old and Middle English. Breton, on the other hand is a variety of South-West Brythonic imported by a relatively small number of speakers into a new environment where it was surrounded by Continental Celtic and Gallo-Latin and later French.

1.2 Unique Phonological Features of Cornish

Indeed, quite apart from the question of orthography, Cornish exhibits phonetic developments that are absent from Breton (and from Welsh also), and which bring into question Loth's assertion that Breton and Cornish are dialects of each other. I list here five separate phonetic features of Middle Cornish that have no equivalent in either of the other Brythonic languages:

1) Short unstressed syllables are reduced to the neutral vowel [ə]; for examples see 1.3 below.
2) Long [iː] finally and in some monosyllables is diphthongized to [əɪ] or [eɪ]; e.g. Cornish *kei* 'dog' but Breton *ki* and Welsh *ci*.
3) Final *-d* and intervocalic *-d-* are assibilated to [z] (written ‹s›) or [dʒ] (written ‹g›, ‹i›, or ‹j›); e.g. Cornish *tas* 'father' but Breton *tad*. The consonant group *-nt-* is similarly assibilated to [nz] or [dʒ]; e.g. Cornish *kerense, kerenge* 'love' but Breton *carantez;* Cornish *dans* 'tooth' but Breton *dant*.
4) Before historic *nn* and *m* a stressed short vowel is in some dialects pre-occluded to [ᵈn] and [ᵇm] respectively—a phenomenon unknown in Breton and Welsh; e.g. Cornish *pedn* but Breton *penn;* Cornish *cabm* 'bent' but Breton *kamm*.
5) At the beginning of a syllable [x] is reduced to [h]; similarly initial [xw] is weakened to [ʍ]. Thus Cornish has *yagh* 'healthy' but *yehes* 'health', which contrasts with Welsh *iach* and *iechyd*, Breton *yac'h* and *yec'hed*. Further Cornish *golgh* 'wash' but *golhy* 'to wash' contrasts with Welsh *golch* and *golchi* and Breton *gwalc'h* and *gwalc'hiñ*.

The items listed in items 3), 4), and 5) above are matters pertaining to the consonant system of Cornish and will be discussed fully at 6.1–7.2, 11.1–11.8, and 12.1-–12.3 below. Items 1) and 2), on the other hand involve the treatment of vowels, and will be discussed briefly here.

1.3 Reduction of Unstressed Syllables in Middle Cornish

Cornish, like both Breton and Welsh, exhibits a metrical system in which unstressed vowels may rhyme with both stressed and unstressed vowels. Unlike the sister languages, however, Cornish shows variation in the quality of its unstressed rhyming vowels. Historically the word *honan* 'self' contains unstressed *a;* cf. Welsh *hunan* 'self'. In *Pascon agan Arluth* it rhymes with *wan* 'weak', *tan* 'take' and *man* 'a bit, at all':

An peynys a wotheuys
ny ve ragtho y ***honan***
lemmyn rag pobyll an bys
pan vons y kefis mar ***wan***
an ioull ȝe adam kewsys
an aval te kemer ***tan***
a vell du y fethyth gurys
pan yn provas nyn io ***man*** (PA §6).

Later in the same poem, however, *honan* is written *honon* and rhymes with *eȝewon* 'Jews', *scon* 'soon', and *don* 'to carry':

Pan o kentrow lemmys
hy as duk ȝen ***eȝewon***
crows Ihesus navnio paris
y eth ȝy laȝe yn ***scon***
bresell cref a ve sordijs
en grows pu elle ȝy ***don***
dre vur stryff y fe Iuggijs
ys degy crist y ***honon*** (PA §160).

In *Beunans Meriasek* the same etymon, spelt *honen*, rhymes with *len* 'faithful':

Syne an grovs kymer genys
ha ty as led del vynneys
poren theth voth ȝe ***honen***
ihesu a vyn da guereys
rag the voys y servont ***len*** (BM 4057-61).

The plural of *flogh* 'child' is spelt *flehas* in *Origo Mundi* (OM) and rhymes with *bras* 'great', *wlas* 'kingdom' and *vas* 'good':

noe dre the thadder ***bras***
ty a vew ov grath nefre
kemer the wrek ha'th ***flehas***
h'aga gvraget gor ganse
a bub eghen best yn ***wlas***
gor genes dew annethe
a bup kynde ethen ***vas***
y'th worhel guet dew gorre (OM 973-80).

Later in the same text, however, the word is spelt *flehys* and rhymes with *trygys* 'settled, dwelling':

the arluth nef ythough druyth
dun alemma the'n mor ruyth
tus venenes ha ***flehys***
the'n tyreth a thythwadow
yw reys gans dev caradow
thyn ena rag vos ***trygys*** (OM 1621-26).

Quite apart from rhymes the labile nature of Middle Cornish unstressed vowels is striking:

'recognize' (original *o*): *aswon* OM 1375, 1488, PC 2416, TH 6; *aswan* TH 11a, 39a; *aswen* BM 73.

'to get' (original *o*): *cafos* PA 38b, 39b, 121b, 164c, 174d, 225d, 234b, OM 388, PC 378; *caffos* PA 149d; *gafos* PC 2455, RD 840; *gaffos* PC 2068; *cafas* BK 542, 926, 1082, 2101, 2250, 3045; *kafas* TH 11; *gafas* TH 36; *cafes* OM 391, 454; *cafus* OM 647, 968, 2071, PC 588, 594, 678, BM 841, 1053, 1251, 2026, TH 13, 16a, 24, 52a; *caffus* OM 1835; *gafus* CF 24, PC 985, 1178, 1531, 2683, TH 3, 13a, 14a, 20a, 24a, 39, 39a x 2; *kafus* OM 471, 497, 750, 1826, 2482, TH 7a, 14a, 19, 21a, 41a x 2, 51a; *gafys* OM 432.

'hard' (original *e*): *calas* OM 1482, 1502, 1564, RD 1086, 2260; *cales* OM 1525, PC 927, 1008, RD 244, 1987, BM 671; *calis* TH 28; *calys* PA 196d, 209d, TH 18, BK 3123, 3167.

'even' (original *o*): *compas* CW 1743; *compes* OM 2494, 2510, CW 492; *compis* TH 21, 26a x 2, BK 239; *compos* OM 2442, 2488; *compys* OM 2455, 2531, 2537, PC 1206, 2736, TH 8a.

'sight' (original *o*): *golak* BK 474, 2343; *golag* BK 304, 1407; *golek* BM 4398; *golok* OM 1530, RD 1861, 1915, BM 3386, BK 752, BM 1559; *goloc* PC 964.

'ship' (original *a*): *gorhal* OM 1050; *gorhel* OM 950, 966, 1146, RD 2323, 2329, BM 468; *gorhyl* OM 1040, 1046, 1063.

'to know' (original *o*): *gothvos*, OM 2098, BK 28; *gothvas* BM 104, BK 320; *wothfes* OM 195

'worn' (original *y*): *guyskys* PC 1780, 2134, 2533, RD 2489; *gweskis* PA 64b; *gweskes* CW 978; *Guesgaz* AB: 248b.

'now' (original *y*): *leman* PC 69, 691, 757, BM 4119, 4143; *lemman* PA 245d, PC 307, 762, RD 246, BM 3542; *lemmen* BM 57, 1335, BK 521, 603; *lemyn* OM 129, 910, PC 410, RD 730, BM 3811; *lemmyn* PA 12c, 15b, 125c, OM 1306, PC 1242, RD 86, BK 235.

'prophet' (original *u*): *profes* PC 562; *profos* PC 2367, RD 66, 1686; *profus* OM 1799, PC 325, 970, RD 1485, 1680; *profys* PC 1923.

The variability of vowels in unstressed syllables is also noteworthy when they are in absolute auslaut and thus unprotected by a final consonant. There are numerous examples of the confusion of unstressed final *-a,-e* and *-o* in the earliest texts. For further examples see CT §§ 7.2-6.

1.4 Development of long [i:] in Middle Cornish

In the later Cornish texts historic /i:/ in absolute final is often written as a diphthong. Here are some examples:

chy 'house': *tshei* BF: 15, 16, 17 x 6, 18 x 5; *Choy* BF: 16, 27; *Tshoy Uûn* BF: 17; *tzhei* BF: 18; *tshyi* BF: 18; *chuy* BF: 42; *Chey* BF: 43; *Chei* BF: 55; *Tshyi* AB: 55c.

cry 'cry' (substantive): *krei* BF: 17 x 3, 18.

dry 'to bring': *drey* PA 21d, 41a; OM 1860.

hy 'she': *hei* BF: 16, 17, 18; *hyi* BF: 19.
ky 'dog': *Kei* AB: 46a, 291a.
ny 'we': *nei* BF: 16 x 2, 17 x 3, 18 x 4, 19, 57.
ry 'to give': *the rey* PC 537; *a rey* PC 2472; *Dho rei* AB: 55b, 117b; *rei* BF: 16 x 2.
try 'three': *tray hans* Borde; *trei* BF: 15 x 2, 17 x 2; *Trey* AB: 230c.
why 'you' (plural): *whay a yll gwelas* TH 33a; *huei* BF: 16, 17 x 2, 19; *whey* BF: 16; *whei* x 3 BF: 55; *wei* BF: 55.

Although diphthongal spellings do not appear for the most part until the Late Cornish period, rhymes indicate that already final long /iː/ (written ‹y›) was pronounced with a diphthong already in Middle Cornish. Here are some examples:

Del yw scrifys prest yma
adro ȝynny gans ***otry***
mara kyll ȝeworth an da
ȝe weȝyll drok agan ***dry***
folle yn ta y whela
ys del wra lyony ***bray***
drey den yn peyn a calla
neffre ny vynsa moy ***ioy*** (PA 21).

In that stanza *dry* 'to bring with an original /iː/ rhymes with *otray* 'outrage', spelt ‹otry›, with *bray*, the lenited form of *pray* 'prey', and *joy* 'joy'. Clearly as early as the period of the composition of PA in the second half of the fourteenth century, long /iː/ had already undergone diphthongization. Notice also that in the penultimate hemistich *dry* itself is spelt ‹drey›, further evidence of this diphthongization.

Further examples of historic long /iː/ rhyming with a diphthong are common, e.g. *ny* 'we' at OM 555 rhyming with *ioy* 'joy' at OM 558; *na moy* 'no more' at OM 946 rhyming with *marnas ty* 'except thee' at OM 948; *ha moy* 'and more' at PC 536 rhyming with *the rey* 'to give' at PC 537 (the spelling *rey* has already been noted above); *dry* 'to bring' at PC 1993 rhyming with *fey* 'faith' at PC 1996; *th'y* 'thither' at RD 185 rhyming with *ioy* 'joy' at RD 186; *na moy* 'no more' at RD 560 rhyming with *gureny ny* 'let us (emphatic)' at RD 561; *asse yllyn ny* 'how we can' at RD 1201 rhyming with *mur ioy* 'much joy' at RD 1202; *mur ioy* 'much joy' at RD 1285 rhyming with *genough why* 'with you (emphatic)' at RD 1286; *fout a ioy* 'lack of joy' at RD 1561 rhyming with *pry* 'earth, clay' at RD 1563; *na moy* 'any more' at RD 2036 rhyming with *the thythyow the gy* 'thy days' (emphatic) at RD 2037; *gruegh ry* 'do give (imperative)' at BM 497 rhyming with *dadder moy* 'more goodness' at BM 499; *ham banneth vy* 'and my blessing (emphatic)' at BM 507 rhyming with *the vay* 'thy kiss' at BM 508; *achy* 'within' at BM 1869 rhyming with *moy* 'more' at BM 1870; *in agen mesk ny* 'among us (emphatic)' BM 1874 rhyming with *kuntel moy* 'collect more' at BM 1877; *the fay* 'thy faith' at BM 2460 rhyming with *thymmo vy* 'to me (emphatic)' at BM 2461; *an fay* 'the faith' at BM 3515 rhyming with *ahanes gy* 'of thee (emphatic)' at BM 3516; *ma hy* 'she is' at BM 4071 rhyming with *ha moy* 'and more' at BM 4072.

Corroborating evidence that diphthongization of historic long /iː/ has already occurred in Middle Cornish is the frequent appearance in the texts of hypercorrect spellings. We know that the vowel of the word for 'three' (feminine) had a diphthong, for Lhuyd writes this as *tair* at AB: 166b and as *Tair* AB: 243c and 248b; he also cites *Tair delkian* 'Three leaves' and *Tair bledhan* 'Three years' both at AB: 243c. Lhuyd's *tair* 'three (feminine)' agrees with the form seen in *tayre sprusan* 'three pips' CW 1845 and *tayr sprusan* 'three pips' CW 1923. An earlier form with *ey* rather than *ai, ay* is seen in *teyr spik* 'three spikes' PC 2370. On the other hand 'Three Maries' are written *tyr marya* PA 230d, 253a and *tyr marea* PA 252b. 'Three trees' appears as *tyr gvethen* at OM 828 and 'three rods' as *tyr guelen* occurs at OM 1945. It seems fair to assume that the spelling *tyr* for *teyr* (later *tayr*) was the result of hypercorrection. The scribe knew that a long *y* in monosyllables often had a diphthongal pronunciation, and thus wrote **tyr* incorrectly for *teyr*.

Further examples of similar hypercorrection are forthcoming. The expected diphthongal form of the word for 'wolf' is seen in Lhuyd's *Blaidh* 'wolf' AB: 82b, 241b, 294b; but the hypercorrect spelling can be seen in *blyth* BM 1104 and *blygh* CW 1149. The second person singular imperative of the verb *treylya* 'to turn' is *treyl* at OM 66, PC 1155 and BM 823. The verbal noun appears in Lhuyd's version of JCH as *trailia* BF: 17 and as *Dho trailia* at AB: 140b and AB: 172c; the third person singular of the preterite is *trailiaz* BF: 18 x 2 and the verbal noun is written *traylyah* and *traylya* by Rowe (ÉCII: 182, 185). Yet the verbal noun is attested as *tryle* PA 15d, 40a, 107d, PC 1293; as *trylye* PA 109d, PC 578, as *trylya* at TH 64a and *trylia* BK 892. Moreover the second person singular imperative is *Tryl* at BK 290. It seems fair to assume that spellings with simple *y* as the stressed vowel are based on the monosyllabic imperative *treyl*, where *tryl* is written by hypercorrection for *treyl*, later *trayl*.

1.5 The Unique Phonological Features of Cornish and the Prosodic Shift

The five features listed at 1.2 are unique to Cornish among the Brythonic languages and do therefore require some explanation. The reduction of unstressed syllables to schwa is reminiscent of the similar phenonomen in Middle English. Indeed in his celebrated 'When did Middle English begin?' of 1930 Malone draws attention to the way in which final unstressed *a, e, o* and *u* are confused in Old English as early as the tenth century. There can be little doubt that the confusion of unstressed vowels in Cornish is related to the similar development in English. As I have suggested elsewhere, it is likely that as a result of the Norman Conquest of England and Cornwall in the late eleventh century, many Anglicized Cornishmen, who had begun to learn and speak English when Cornwall was dominated by the West Saxons, began to relearn

Cornish. This would have been for several reasons. In the first place, in the generations immediately after the Conquest English was replaced by Norman French as the language of the ruling elite and of administration. Secondly a relatively large influx of Bretons into Cornwall enhanced links between Cornwall and its Brythonic relatives across the sea. This seems have had cultural repercussions leading ultimately to the founding of a Cornish language scriptorium in Glasney and to practice of composing and performing religious plays in Cornish. It should be remembered that the Cornish plays, the *Ordinalia* and the two serviving saints' lives, *Beunans Meriasek* and *Bewnans Ke* are reminiscent of Breton models, rather than the mystery plays of Middle English. The Old Cornish Vocabulary, which probably dates from the early eleventh century, is perhaps the first evidence we have for a Cornish revival after the Norman Conquest. The English entries in an original Latin-English vocabulary were translated into Cornish presumably to assist those Cornish Anglophones who were now anxious to improve their knowledge of Cornish. Since, however, some, if not all, of these English speakers would have been more fluent in English than in Cornish, it is probably not astonishing that their relearnt Cornish exhibited a strong English substratum. The weakening of unstressed syllables a distinctive feature of this English influence.

The diphthongization of original long /iː/ is another feature that can be ascribed to the adoption of English speech habits into Cornish. We know from Modern Welsh that unstressed syllables retained much of their sonority; and we also know from Modern Welsh and Modern Breton that stressed syllables can either be long or short. The same was probably true of Cornish. With the penetration of English speech habits into Cornish, stressed vowels would have have shortened somewhat but correspondingly would have beeen pronounced with greater vigour than previously. In polysyllables this would have meant the reduction of unstressed syllables to schwa, which has been discussed at 1.3 above. In stressed monosyllable with a vowel in absolute auslaut this Anglicization of pronunciation would also have had far reaching results. Before the Norman Conquest a long monosyllable would have been three morae in length, whereas a long vowel in a disyllable would have contained two morae. Thus, for example, the monosyllabic word *ky* 'dog' would schematically have been *[kiii] or *[ki·i], where [i·] represents a vowel of two morae. When Cornish phonology came under the influence of English, the half-long first element in *[ki·i] would have reduced from three morae to two. As it did so the first element in the vowel would have become less tense. It would thus have opened to [ɪ]: *[ki·i > kii > kɪi]. At this point the nucleus [ɪ] of the erstwhile trimoric vowel would have been lower than the coda [i]. The two parts would have continued to move apart, giving [kəɪ], written ‹kei›.

Wakelin suggests that long /iː/ in Cornish was 'assimilated' to late Middle English long *ī* 'and took part to some extent in its further development' (Wakelin: 83). This is highly unlikely, because it assumes that this long vowel of Middle Cornish underwent one aspect of a change in another language, namely the Great Vowel Shift. The Great Vowel Shift involved a wholesale reordering of the vocalic system of Middle English in which a group of changes depended on each other. It is hardly likely that an unrelated language, Cornish, would undergo one part only of this fullscale restructuring. Nor does Wakelin offer any explanation why Cornish /iː/ uniquely should follow English, when other vowels did not. At all events Wakelin's conjecture cannot possibly be correct, since, as we have noted, Cornish *y* in *dry* was rhyming with *joy* 'joy' and *pray* 'prey' already in *Pascon agan Arluth* in the fourteenth century at a time when the Great Vowel Shift had only just begun. Wakelin is correct, however, in assuming that the diphthongization of Cornish [iː] > [əɪ] was due to the influence of English. Such influence, however, was more indirect than Wakelin's suggested development.

The two changes listed above under 3) and 4) above, i.e. the assibilation of *d* and *nt* and the pre-occlusion of *m* and *n* to *bm* and *dn* respectively can also be shown to be as a result of penetration into Cornish of English speech habits. I will discuss these phenomena in Chapters 6, 7, and 11 respectively. It should be noted, however, that it is clear that 5) in the above list is a development which owes its origins to English. In Middle English [x] written ‹gh› could stand at the end of a syllable, e.g. in *plough*. It was unknown at the beginning of a syllable, however. In both Welsh and Breton [x], written ‹ch› in Welsh and ‹c'h› in Modern Breton can stand at the beginning of a syllable, e.g. Welsh *ei chalon* 'her heart', Breton *e c'halon* 'her heart' but Cornish *y holon* 'her heart' PA 122c, 164b; *hy holon* PA 224b, OM 2174, 2748. Similarly the Welsh for 'bitter', for example, is *chwerw* and the Breton is *c'hwerv*. The Cornish, on the other hand, is *wherow* RD 2601. *Chwant* is the Welsh for 'desire', and *c'hoant* is the Breton equivalent. The Cornish, however, is *whans* PA 1b, OM 91, RD 1330, CW 1910. It is noteworthy that [xw] is unknown in syllable initial in English, but [ʍ] is common.

1.6 Terminology

In previous works I have referred to the shift from Old Cornish to a more anglicized pronunciation in Middle Cornish as the Prosodic Shift. This term refers to the way in which long and half-long syllables were shortened in the period after the Norman Conquest, when Middle English speech habits began to affect the phonology of Cornish. The present work deals largely with the effects of the same phenomenon on the consontal system of Cornish. It is still the Prosodic Shift (PS) but in the discussion below it will be seen that its effects are wider than simply on the vocalic system of the language.

CHAPTER 2

Final *k* / *g* and *p* / *b* in monosyllables

2.1 Final *k/g* and *p/b* in monosyllables

One of the least satisfactory aspects of Unified Cornish is the way in which the orthography never decided the exact nature of the final segment in such words as *brak* / *brag* 'malt'; *gwak* / *gwag* 'empty, hungry'; *rak* / *rag* 'for'; *gwrek* / *gwreg* 'wife'; *tek* / *teg* 'beautiful, fair'; *whek* / *wheg* 'sweet'; *drok* / *drog* 'evil'; *fok* / *fog* 'hearth, furnace'; *gwruk* / *gwrug* 'did, made'; *kyk* / *kyg* 'flesh'; *map* / *mab* 'son'; *hep* / *heb* 'without'; *nep* / *neb* 'any, some'; *glyp* / *glyb* 'wet'; and *typ* / *tyb* 'considers'. On the other hand Unified Cornish usually has no hesitation in writting ‹k› and ‹p› respectively after unstressed vowels, e.g. *carrek, boghosek, uthyk, modryp, hevelep, gorthyp*, etc.

In order to determine the phonetic value of these final stops in the traditional language, it might be helpful in the first instance to collect the available instances of some sample etyma from the texts.

2.2 *k* and *g* after stressed vowels

1) 'empty, hungry'
gvak OM 365, 593, BM 3927.
gwag CW 1172, ACB: F f *verso; gwage* ÉCII: 186; *Guâg* AB: 57c, 169a.

2) 'woman, wife'
gwrek PA 66c, BK 653; *gurek* PA 158a; *gruek* RD 2227, BM 302, 2508, 2786; *gvrek* OM 265, 386, 708, 1036, PC 557; *wrek* CF 10, PA 66b, 122b, 157c, OM 312, 346, 932, 975, 1159, 2245, PC 685, 1920, RD 901.
gwreg CF 13, TH 7, 8; *gwreag* CW 877; *gwreage* LAM: 230; *wreag* CW 976, 1451, 1454, 2227, 2252, 2476, 2540, BF 16 x 3; *'wreag* BF: 16; *wreage* CW 834, 966; *Wreag* BF: 15; *gwrêg* BF: 55; *gwreg* BF: 55; *gwrege* Bilbao; *Greage* LAM: 230; *urêg* BF: 16; *gurêg* AB: 60c, 95b, 295a; *Gurêg* AB: 14c, 179b, 241c; *An urêg* AB: 241c; *an urêg-na* AB: 243c.

3) 'fair, beautiful
tek PA 13d, 44d, 71d, 161a, 177c, 244b, OM 87, 141, 267, 552, 753, 769, 1147, 1170, 1203, 1450, 2080, 2155, 2198, 2441, 2446, 2462, PC 36, 258, 415, 818, 1294, 2538, RD 1659, 2617, BM 21, 69, 200, 748, 914, 1409, 1411, 1424, 1497, 1519, 1574, 1851, 2006, 2134, 2624, 2806, 3069, 3144, 3824, 4019, 4256, 4336, 4421, 4442, BK 656, 1021, 2062, 3306, KG1; *teke* CW 94, 112, 452, 1051.

teg TH 3a, CW 947; *têg* BF: 16, 17, AB: 50b, 65c, 243c, 149a, 243c; *Têg* AB: 41c, 42c,53c, 61a, 65c, 132a, 152c, LAM: 244, ACB: F f, CPR: 11; *teag* ACB: F f 2c *verso* x 5; *Teage* BF: 38.

4) 'sweet, dear'

whek PA 47b, 66b, 77d, 171a, 185c, 222c, 232a, 244c, OM 446, 451, 479, 525, 533, 615, 770, 1135, 1336, 1345, 1715, 1743, 1813, 1994, 2074, 2132, 2175, 2195, 2255, 2258, 2329, 2459, 2509, 2791, PC 35, 589, 704, 753, 989, 1031, 1041, 1291, 1435, 1447, 1637, 1735, 1847, 1895, 2331, 2337, 2773, 2949, 3016, 3055, 3155, RD 430, 447, 471, 736, 1482, 1639, 1755, 2087, BM 158, BK 13, 1019, 1373, 2049, 2060, 2893; *wek* OM 166, BM 24, 53, 66, 87, 114, 286, 298, 329, 347, 424, 527, 714, 749, 911, 1329, 1577, 1653, 2344, 2676, 2758, 2763, 3119, 3178, 3194, 4031, 4097, 4195, 4249, 4558.

wheg TH 2, 27a x 2, 28; *whêg* CPR: 9; *whege* BF: 38; *wheag* CW 95, ACB: F f 2 *verso* x 5; *wheage* ACB: F f, F f 2 *verso*, BF: 39; *Wheage* LAM: 238; *Huêg* AB: 4c, 26a, 88a, 156c, 287b; *huêg* AB: 47c, 56a.

5) 'flesh'

kyk OM 112, 659, PC 2941, BM 2028, 3066, 3085, 4054, 4191, BK 365, 790, 1273, 1289.

kyg PA 3b, 54b, 256d, TH 52, SA 61 x 2, 65a, BK 2280, CW 2222; *kyge* TH 3 x 2, 9a, 15, 16a x 4, 27a, 44, 51a, 52, 54, 56 x 2, 57a; *kig* SA 60 x 2, 61 x 2, 61a, 62; *kigg* SA 60a x 7, 61 x 2, 62 x 2, 63a x 2, 64a x 4, 65a, 66 x 2; *kigge* SA 59.

2.3 *k* and *g* after unstressed vowels

1) 'poor'

bohosek BM 438, 693, 736, 877, 1779, 2167, 2183, 2695, 2939, 3103, 4250; *bothosek* BM 328; *vohosek* BM 3120; *bohosak* BK 773; *behosek* TH 6a; *Bohodzack* BF: 43, 44; *boadjack* Bodinar; *Bohosak* AB: 231a; *Bohozek* AB: 268a; *bohodzhak* AB: 231a; *Bohodzhak* AB: 71b, 115a, 230b; *vohozhak* AB: 243c.

There are no instances with final ‹g›.

2) 'rock'

carrek BM 1072; *garrek* BM 1016; *karrek* BM 1024; *carrak* TH 45a x 2; *karrack* BF: 25, 27; *garrak* OM 2464, TH 44, 45a x 2; *garrack* TH 44; *Garrack* BF: 43, 44.

There are no instances with final ‹g›.

3) 'twelve'

dewthek OM 1060, PC 228; *dewthack* CW 1981, 1984; *dowȝek* PA 47a, 61a; *dowthak* BK 1434, LAM 244; *douthak* Bilbao; *douthack* Bilbao; *Dowthack* ACB: F f 2.

There are no instances with final ‹g›.

4) 'powerful'

gallosek OM 1494, 2089, PC 157, 165, RD 118, 122, 752, 1168, 1906, 2394, BM 179; *gallogek* RD 2376; *olgallogak* BK 218; *galosek* RD 108, 1334, BM 179, 300, 349, 441, 1096, 1330, 1782, 1944, 1975, 2114, 2121, 2129, 2188, 2224, 2526, 2620, 2932, 3081, 3088, 4384, 4424; TH 12a, 35, 54, 54a; *gallosack* RCEV: 99; *galosak* BK 1400, 1997; *gollousacke* CW 13.

There are no instances with final ‹g›.

5) 'sight'

golok OM 1530, RD 1861, 1915; BM 3386, BK 752, 992; *wolok* PC 2100; *golek* BM 4398; *golak* BK 474, 2343; *woolak* KG1.

golog BK 570, 3183; *golag* BK 304, 1407, 3188.

6) 'big-eyed; observant person'

lagasek BM 1018, 3813; *lagajak* BK 210, 369; *Lagadzhak* AB: 105b; cf. *kabmlagadzhak* AB: 155b & *Ydnlagadzhak* AB: 93c

There are no instances with final ‹g›.

7) 'joyful'

lowenek PA 244d, 257a, OM 449, 549, 833, RD 1333, 1418, 1849, 1905, BM 277, 353, 582, 1852, 2716, 4434, TH 49a; *lowenake* CW 546; *Louenak* AB: 75b; *lawanneck* Carew: 127.

There are no instances with final ‹g›.

8) 'doctor'

methek RD 1632, 1648, BM 731, 2528, 4394; *vethek* BM 4245; *vethak* BK 805, 825; *medhek* AB: 47c; *medhik* AB: 240c.

metheg TH 11, *methag* TH 25a.

9) 'horseman'

marhek PA 241d, 242a, 244a, 245a, OM 2004, 2139, 2150, 2204, 2226, 2338, BM 350, 2444; *Marrak* PA 246a, BK 1648; *marrak* BK 1514, 1632; *Marhak* AB: 240c.

marreg PA 190b x 2, 217a , 218b; *Marhag* AB: 57a.

10 'prince'
pensevyk BM 489, 3022, 3209; *pensevik* SA 66; *pensevike* SA 60a.

There are no instances with final ‹g›.

11) 'dreadful'
vthek OM 798; *vtheck* CW 290; *vthyk* PC 952, RD 531, 2340, BM 729; *uthicke* CW 486; *Eithick* ACB: F f 3; *ithik* AB: 68a, 102a, 120c, 122b, 155c, 169a; *ithick* AB: 76c.
Ithig AB: 249a.

2.4 *p* and *b* after stressed vowels
There are fewer etyma ending in *p* / *b* than in *k*/*g* and the suitable monosyllables are so common in the texts, that not every instance is listed below:

1) 'without'
hep PA 138c, OM 124, 130, 207, 236, 240, 251, 252, 259, 264, 278, 302, 428, 466, 484, 497, 548, 558, 569, 631, 639, 659, 724, 777, 798, 825, 871, 877, 974, 999, 1037, etc., PC 8, 30, 34, 42, 64, 65, 130, 175, 186, 240, 286, 301, 466, 498, 559, 591, 600, 618, 665, 678, 728, 754, 827, 909, 914, 945, 968, 983. etc., RD 6, 15, 50, 83, 88, 101, 110, 116, 160, 221, 228, 286, 317, 319, 323, 324, 367, 461, 564, 637, 654, 738, 798, 974, 1030, 1094, 1237, 1293, 1421, 1586, 1587, 1619, 1623, 1644, 1695, 1748, 1752, 1822, 1834, 1860, 1891, etc., BM 1153, 3337, BK 1269, 2109, 2755, BF: 25, 29.
heb PA 12a, 56c, 73d, 76c, 80d, 83d, 91c, 98c, 116b, 127b, 139b, 165d, 174b, 178b, 192c, 197b, 203a, 204b, 208d, 212d, 235b, 235c, 248c, 252c, OM 95, 198, RD 2605, BM 12, 190, 196, 231, 262, 417, 431, 518, 549, 694, 712, 762, 769, 812, 845, 847, 854, 857, 878, 968, 1038, 1042, 1052, 1081, 1155, 1189, 1539, 1617, 1634, 1669, 1718, 1731, 1794, 1805, 1919, 1942, 2036, 2119, 2209, 2233, 2249, 2268, 2275, 2282, 2286, 2492, 2571, 2610, 2688, 2861, 2920, 2921, 2936, 3044, 3068, 3078, 3167, etc., TH 2a, 4, 5 x 3, 7, 7a, 8, 10, 10a x 3, 11, 11a, 12, 13a x 3, 14 x 2, 16 x 2, 19 x 2, 20 x 2, 21, 22a x 2, 23 x 2, 24a, 25, 26, 29a, 30 x 2, 30a, 31a, 33, 35, 37, 38a, 39a, 40a x 3, 41, 46, 47, 50, 50a, 51, 52a, 54, 54a, 57, 59, SA 63, 63a, 66, 66a, BK 20, 55, 72, 79, 114, 153, 172, 184, 234, 249, 278, 289, 294, 315, 336, 340, 380, 396, 483, 550, 592, 645, 658, 715, 757, 825, 872, 882, 890, 901, 1028, 1077, 1330, 1335, etc., CW 2, 58, 66, 79, 107, 113, 130, 186, 250, 286, 338, 383, 462, 516, 535, 536, 686, 711, 854, 855, 869, 875, 886, 899, 1077, 1092, 1274, 1321, 1416, 1525, 1629, 1733, 1784, 1898, 1904, 1919, 1983, 1986, 1990, 2020, 2073, 2080, 2096, 2098, 2108, 2147, 2195, 2204, 2250, 2280, 2307, Bodewryd x 2; BF: 9, 12, 39, 46, 51 x 3, 55, 57, LAM: 238, ACB: E e 4, E e 4 *verso*, F f.

2) 'son'

map PA 199d, OM 4, 55, 58, 85, 607, 615, 639, 1321, 1325, 1357, 1380, 1393, 1934, 2347; PC 60, 65, 99, 153, 253, 271, 403, 423, 425, 962, etc., RD 23, 271, 307, 428, 442, 447, 463, 479, 630, 819, 858, etc., BM 24, 62, 136, 238, 329, 345, 362, 363, 381, 486, 508, 527, 552, 781, 871, 887, 1125, 1146, etc., TH 20, BK 2304.

mab PA 1a, 3b, 7a, 8d, 9c, 11c, 12a, 14d, 19b, 23b, 52a, 54a, 58c, 95d, 100d, 122a, 129c, 143b, 164c, 165a, 171b, 197b, 197d, 208d, 210d, 221b, 223a, 226d, 227d, 231a, 252d, 259a, OM 13, 565, 809, 1950, PC 2724, BM 9, 35, 53, 157, 1128, 3163, TH 1 x 3, 2, 3 x 2, 4, 4a, 5a, 7 x 2, 10a, 12a, 15, 16, 26, 30, 41, 43 x 3, 43a, 44, 45a, 46, 47, 50a, 51, BK 170, 308, 718, 781, 1030; 1056, 1124, 1282, 1327, 1403, 1641, 1707, 1782, 1804, 1834, 1882, 2081, 2164, 2319, 2895; 3305, CW 254, 344, 1278, 1601; *Mab* BK 5, 226, 233, 236, 240, 264, 789, 824, 2900, BF: 27, 46, 48; *mâb* ÉCII: 191; *mâbe* ÉCII: 186; *mabe* CW 9, 1059, 1060, 1164, 1252, 1254, 1323, 1395, 1397, 1434, 1436, 1501, 1510, 1516, 1597, 1670, 1727, 1757, 1943, 1952, 1983, 2096, 2149, 2220, 2232, 2340, 2473, 2518, 2539; *maab* ÉCII: 187.

2.5 *p* and *b* after unstressed vowels

1) 'answer' (substantive)

gorthyp PC 512, 1839; RD 1851, TH 29a.

gorthyb BM 1442, BK 211, 2094, 2101, 2140, 2274; *worthyb* BK 604, 2263, 3168; CW 1198, 1736, 1761; *worthib* CW 265; *gurryb* TH 13a; *orybe* SA 62.

2) 'answer' (3 sg. pres.-fut. & 2 sg. imper.)

gorthyp PC 1722, 1735, 2008, RD 494, 1228, 1834; *worthyp* PC 1237, 1751, 1973, 2803

gorthyb BM 3547, BK 150, 199, 1887; *worthyb* BK 52, 192, 1876, 2099; *gortheb* OM 2229; *wortheb* OM 2235, ACB: E e 4 *verso.*

3) 'bishop'

epscop OM 2601, 2614, 2655, 2731, 2750, 2757, 2773, 2777, PC 361, 931, 1129, 1134, 1201, 1353, 1794, 1851, 2344, BM 511, 519, 575, 896, 1379, 1391,1394, 1434, 2687, 2691, 2697, 2702, 2708, 2712, 2727, 2760, 2809, 2819, 2860, 2869, 2874, 2884, 2888, 2890, 2906, 2909, 2952, 2958, 2999, 3005, 3021, 3902, 3915, TH 47a, 48a x 2, 49, 50, 50a; *Epscop* BM 1486, TH 33a, 46a, 49, 50a; *ispak* AB: 7c, 57a.

epscob PC 572, TH 39 x 3, 47a.

4) 'likeness'

hevelep OM 2337, BM 2150, TH 1a x 2, 5, 28a, 55 x 2, 55a, SA 66a, AB: 230c.

heveleb TH 1a x 4, 2a, 44a.

The alternation of *p* ~ *b* after an unstressed syllable can hardly be ascribed to sandhi, i.e. to the phonetic shape of the initial segment of the following word. This can be seen from the following *kettep pen* 'each one' at OM 1655, PC 462, 762, 1796, 2513, 2769 and 3048 is always so spelt where *kettep* precedes [p] and *kettep onan* 'each one' appears at PC 2231, 2251, 2500, 2700, 2801, 2814, 2821, 2856 and 3071, where *kettep* precedes a vowel.

2.6 The phonetic value of final *k*/*g* and *p*/*b*

The Celtic scribal tradition in both Britain and Ireland was based upon the British pronunciation of Latin. It tended therefore to write voiced *g* and *b* as *c* / *k* and *p* in final position. This can be seen in such spellings as MW *gureic*, MC *gwrek* 'woman, wife'; MW *goruc*, MC *gwruk* 'did, made'; MW *cic, kic*, OC *chic*, MC *kyk* 'flesh'; MW *chwec*, MC *whek* 'sweet, pleasant'; MW *karrec*, MC *carrek* 'rock'; MW *medyc*, MC *methek* 'doctor'; MW *hep*, MC *hep* 'without' and MW *escop*, MC *epscop* 'bishop'. There are notable exceptions to this pattern, however. *Mab* 'son' is usually so spelt in early Welsh, and *mab* occurs three times in OCV, where *map* is unknown; *mab* occurs 33 times in PA, but *map* once only.

In later Welsh and later Cornish in stressed monosyllables the two voiced consonants were written *g* and *b* respectively: W *gwraig*, C *gwreg*; W *chweg*, C *wheg*; W *heb*, C *heb*. In Welsh earlier *c* and *p* were also replaced by *g* and *b* in disyllables and polysyllables where *g* and *b* were preceded by an unstressed vowel, *carreg* 'rock', *meddyg* 'doctor' and *esgob* 'bishop'. In Cornish for the most part the final segment continued to be written as *k* or *p* after an unstressed vowel. Judging by Lhuyd's phonetic renderings of such items, the final segment was not merely written as ‹k› or ‹p› but was phonetically unvoiced as well.

The devoicing of final *g* and *b* (written ‹k› and ‹p›) after an unstressed vowel is to be ascribed to the same set of developments as those outlined in 1.2. As a result of influence from English after the Norman Conquest, unstressed syllables in Cornish lost much of their sonority. This can be seen in the way in which unstressed vowels tended to be reduced to schwa (see 1.3). It appears that this weakly pronounced neutral vowel was insufficient to maintain the voicing of the following segment. As a result the final *g* and *b* were devoiced to *k* and *p*. This contrasts with the position of unstressed syllables in Welsh, which maintain a high degree of sonority. In Welsh the vocalic quality of the unstressed vowel is not lost and the vowel itself is often pronounced often with noticeably higher tone than the preceding stressed syllable.

There are exceptions to this rule in Cornish of [g], [b] after stressed vowels, and [k], [p] after unstressed ones. The most striking are *marhek* and *gorthyp* (see above), where such spellings as *marreg* and *gorthyb*, *gorryb* are well attested. *Marreg* developed from a from **marheg*, where the internal segment was [r̥], a voiceless *r*. It seems fair to assume that orignal *gorthyb* developed as *gorhyb* (cf. *gurryb* TH 13a) also with a medial voiceless *r*. In both cases we can assume that the devoicing of the final *g* or *b* was blocked by dissimilation. The voiceless *r* in the preceding syllable caused the final consonant of the unstressed syllable to retain its voicing. The presence of *-th-* after the first syllable (possibly to be understood as [h], cf. *bothosek* BM 328 for *bohosek*) may also explain the voiced final in *cotheneb* 'antiquity' at TH 34a and 49.

There are isolated examples elsewhere of a voiced final where an unvoiced consonant might be expected, for example in the following items listed above: *methag* 'doctor', *golog, golag* 'sight', *epscob* 'bishop' and *heveleb* 'likeness'. These instances are sporadic only, since *golog, golag* occur alongside *golok* and *golak* in BK; similarly *epscob* is less common in TH than *epscop,* and *heveleb* is also less common in TH than *hevelep.* Further instances of *g* and *b* for expected *k* and *p* can be seen in *folneb* 'folly' BK 281, *rowndenab* 'roundness' BK 283, *nownsag* 'nineteen' TH 1 (contrast *noundzhak* AB: 176b) and *dyag* 'lazy' TH 2a (contrast *mar thyek* 'so lazy' BM 3360). These examples of voiced consonants can probably be ascribed to hypercorrection. The scribes knew, particularly in the later Middle Cornish period that *g* and *b* were being written in *gwreg, teg, neb, heb,* etc. in preference to earlier *gwrek, tek, nep, hep,* etc. It is not improbable therefore that they sometimes wrote *g* and *b* for *k* and *p* after an unstressed syllable.

Overall however it would seem that by the sixteenth century, Middle Cornish scribes were writing *g* and *b* after a final stressed vowel, and *k* and *p* after an unstressed one. Since this distribution of *g* ~ *k* and *p* ~ *b* was systematic, one should also expect to find a similar picture with *dh* ~ *th* and *v* ~ *f.* These two alternations will be discussed below in Chapters 3 and 4.

2.7 The words for 'cripple' and 'loving' in Cornish

Corroboration of the idea that [k] occurs after unstressed vowels and [g] after stressed ones can be seen in the Cornish reflexes of the word for 'cripple'. The basic form is *efreth,* W *efrydd* < British **amriyos.* With the addition of the adjectival suffix *-ek* one gets a derivative *efrethek* 'crippled, maimed' at BM 540, 564, 684, 4520. The internal segment written ‹th› is voiced [ð]. When it is lost, the final syllable is elided to give a disyllable stressed on the final syllable. This appears as *effreg* [e'fre:g] at TH 44a x 2, 57a x 2. The final segment now follows a stressed long vowel and in consequence is voiced and thus written ‹g›.

Contrast the development of *effrethek* > *effreg* with that of **kerengethek* 'loving' where *-th-* is voiced [ð]. The intervocalic [ð] is lost, but the last two syllables remain distinct and are not elided. As a result the final *k* always occurs after an unstressed vowel. The attested forms are *kerengeak* TH 2a, 10a, 11a; *kerngeek* TH 3, *kyrngeak* 4a and *kernsyak* TH 41 and in each case the final segment is voiceless, i.e. [k].

CHAPTER 3

The alternation of *θ* ‹th› and *ð* ‹dh›

3.1 Were θ‹th› and ð ‹dh› distinct phonemes?

It has been suggested that [θ] (written ‹th› by Lhuyd) and [ð] (written ‹dh› by Lhuyd) were not distinct phonemes in Cornish (Mills 1999: 204). The evidence cited is based on variant spellings by Lhuyd of the same word, e.g. *Forth* and *Fordh* 'road', *Dêdh* and *Deth* 'day', *Kidniadh* and *Kidniath* 'autumn', for example. It should be remembered, however, that Lhuyd both cites manuscript spellings at one moment and at the next respells words according to preconceptions based upon his native Welsh. The pair *Forth* and *Fordh* are a good example. *Forth* is the spelling Lhuyd found in Cornish manuscripts, whereas *Fordh* is his own respelling of it on the basis of W *ffordd* 'way, road'. Lhuyd is unlikely to have heard either, for in his own day the word was [vor], which he spells ‹vòr› at JCH § 6 x 2 and § 16. (For the variation *Kidniadh* ~ *Kidniath* see 4.6 below).

It is very likely nonetheless that for Lhuyd's [θ] and [ð] are indeed different, for he distinguishes the two when they occur in similar environments, for example:

Tethan 'teat' AB: 3b, 84c, 170a, 240c but *Do tedha* 'to melt' AB: 54a
Dyuetha 'last' AB: 175c but *diskuedha* 'to show' AB: 70a
Guetha 'worst' AB: 243b but *Guedhan* 'tree' AB: 10c, 18c, 51c, 84c, etc.
ithik 'terrible' AB: 68a, 102a, etc., but *Bidhyz* 'drowned' AB: 248b, *bidhis* 'id.' AB: 250a
ʒotha 'ought' AB: 250b but *Dho kodha* 'to fall' AB: 45a.

Perhaps the best evidence we have for the Cornish spoken in Lhuyd's day is to be found in JCH at AB: 251-53 (also in BF: 16-9), since this is a continuous text written down, it seems, from dictation. Here Lhuyd distinguishes final [θ] and [ð] in monosyllables or final stressed syllables, writing ‹ꞇ› or ‹th› for [θ], and ‹ꝺ› or ‹dh› for [ð]. In JCH we read:

meꝺ 'said' §§ 2, 4 x 2, 5, 6 x 3, 8 x 3, 9, 10 x 3, 11, 12, 32 x 2, 33 x 2, 34, 42 x 3, 44; *mêꝺ* §§ 7, 8, 24, 43; *ameꝺ* §§ 14, 20, 21, 22, 24, 26, 30, 41; *a meꝺ* § 31; *Ameꝺ* § 15.
vêꝺ 'will be' §§15, 20, 24

ꝺêꞇ 'came' §§ 29, 41
uîꞇ 'care' §§ 6, 8
auêꞇ 'also' § 18.

Notice also that we have a minimal pair in *vêð* 'will be' and *vêτ* 'any'. The first occurs in *ha uelkom ti a vêð* AB: 252:15; *ha uelkŷm tî a vêð* AB: 252:20; and *ha uelkym tî a vêð* AB: 252:24. The second, *vêth* occurs in *Ni vr dên vêth* 'No man at all knows' AB: 244c and *Nag ez triụath vêth dho vi* 'I do not at all pity' AB: 244c.

I think we can be quite sure that [θ] ‹th› and [ð] ‹dh› were distinct phonemes in Cornish.

3.2 *Ethom, othem* 'need'

It is clear from such pairs as *gwetha* 'worst' ~ *gwethen, guedhan* 'tree' that intervocalic ‹th› in Middle Cornish orthography can represent either a voiceless or a voiced consonant. The word *ethom* 'need' PA 155c, OM 967, PC 182, etc., has a variant with vocalic metathesis, *othem* BM 354, 880, 4109, *otham* BK 454, 2358, CW 1132. In Breton the congener of this word is spelt *ezhomm* 'besoin', where *zh* indicates that the medial segment was originally *-th-*. Jackson, however, has drawn attention to forms in the Breton dialects that suggest that the medial consonant might originally have been voiced (HPB: 655-56). He also proposes OIr *adamnae* 'hunger' as a possible congener of the Breton word, although the existence of *adamnae* is uncertain. We have no certain evidence concerning the history of the Cornish forms *ethom, othem*. It should be noted that in his 'Modern Cornish' version of the Ten Commandments Pryce gives: *Na ra chee kymeraz hanno a'n Arleth de Dew heb* ***otham****, ragan Arleth na vedn sinzhy e dipeh, nes es komeres e hanno engwag* 'Thou shalt not take the name of the Lord thy God without necessity, for the Lord will not hold him sinless who takes his name emptily' ACB: E e 3 *verso*. John Boson's translation of this commandment is as follows: *Na re'au kamer Hanow guz Arleth Deiu en Ganow heb* ***ortham****. Rag na vedn an Arleth sendg'e heb Pe, ra kamer'e hanow en ganow heb* ***ortham*** 'You shall not take the name of your Lord God in your mouth without necessity. For the Lord will not hold without sin who will take his name in his mouth without necessity' BF: 55. The manuscript in which this verse is found was written by William Gwavas. Moreover the same form *Ortham* occurs twice more in the Gwavas MSS in a different version of the Ten Commandments also in the the hand of William Gwavas (see RC 24: 5, 6). Four instances of the same word would seem to imply that *ortham* is not a slip, but a genuine form. Indeed Gendall includes *ortham* as a variant of *otham* 'necessity' in his SDMC. It is perhaps more likely that *ortham* < *otham* has been reshaped by popular etymology, perhaps through the idea that necessity comes 'upon me' (**ortham*). If, as seems likely, *ortham* is genuine, the medial segment of the original word *otham* was voiceless, otherwise popular reshaping *otham* > *ortham* could not have occurred. In which case *ethom, othem* are probably more authentic than **edhom, *odhem*.

3.3 Final ‹th› after an unstressed vowel

If *dh* and *th* were phonemically distinct in Cornish, we might perhaps expect to find that their distribution is similar to that of *g* and *k*. We would expect to find *dh* after a stressed vowel (where Welsh has *dd*, e.g. in *bydd* 'will be', *dydd* 'day') and *th* after an unstressed vowel (where Welsh also has *dd*, e.g. in *mynydd* 'mountain', *gwirionedd* 'truth'). Unfortunately the evidence is ambiguous. This is partially because Lhuyd had a tendency to assimilate Cornish words to his native Welsh, rewriting *-eth* in the Cornish texts as *-edh*. It is also partly because unstressed *-eth* from earlier *-edh* had already developed further as *-eth* > *-e*, *-a*.

Lhuyd gives the following plurals: *Abesteledh* 'apostles' AB: 243a, *Guragedh* 243a, and *Eledh* 'angels' AB: 249b. He continues, however, by saying that such plurals are no longer used in speech —which means that he had never heard them. He says of his putative plural ending **-edh* ending:

> It's at present changed into *-es* according to their writing; but into *-ez* according to their Pronunciation. So that it seems a sort of French or modern English plural; as *Bestez*, Beasts; *Koles*, Coals; *Romes*, Rooms; *gules*, Guls; *Pysgez*, Fish; *Panez*, Parsnips; *Zilliez*, Eels or Congers; *Lahez*, Laws; *Benenez*, Women; †*Flexez*, children (AB: 243a).

Lhuyd is confusing various plural formations in that paragraph. *Pysgez* for example is for OC **puscot* and *Benenez* for OC **benenet*, *Flexez* for OC *flechet* and *Zilliez* for OC **silliet*, all with final assibilated dentals. *Bestez*, *Kolez*, *Romes* and *Lahez* have plurals based on Middle English *-es*. We can safely deduce from that remark of Lhuyd's that he never actually heard *-edh* [eð] used as a plural ending in Cornish. This is not astonishing, since by his time one would expect *-edh* (W *-edd*) to have become *-eth*, if it had not already developed further to final [ə].

Lhuyd also on occasion writes *-edh* in other words. Under *Veracitas* 'truth' at AB: 171c Lhuyd gives the Cornish as †*Guirionedh*. The dagger preceding the entry implies that the word has been respelt from Old Cornish, although the word is not actually found in OCV. In the introduction to his grammar of Cornish Lhuyd spells the word for 'truth' as *guironeth* AB 222 with a voiceless final consonant. This looks more authentic than *Guirionedh*, for several reasons. The form cited at AB: 171c is identical with the Welsh form in the preceding line. On the other hand the form *guironeth* at AB: 222 lacks the second *i*, and is similar therefore to forms attested elsewhere in Cornish (e.g. *guyroneth* OM 702, 740, PC 735, 760). The same word spelt *Gwyroneth* is also cited by Lhuyd at AB: 240c along with *Skiantoleth* 'prudence', *Folneth* 'folly', *Banneth* 'blessing', *Kyzoleth* 'peaceableness', *Bolonegeth* 'will' and *Gouegneth* 'fraud'. Only one of these items has an immediate W congener: *banneth* 'blessing', which is identical in origin with W *bendith* (‹ Latin *benedictio*) with a voiceless final. Although *skiantoleth* has no immediate Welsh relative, abstract nouns in *-olaeth*, e.g. *mamolaeth* 'maternity', *marwolaeth* 'death', *tadolaeth* 'paternity', etc., are not uncommon and they have a final voiceless consonant. Since Lhuyd lists them together with *banneth* as ending in the same desinence *-eth*, *skiantoleth* and *kyzoleth* can also be considered to end in a voiceless final. We must also assume therefore that Lhuyd here, at least, believed the final segment in *gwyroneth* to be voiceless also.

Lhuyd's *Guirionedh* is by analogy with W *gwirionedd;* his more authentic *Guironeth* at AB: 222, 223 and 240c is to be understood as ending in *-eth,* not *-edh. Cosoleth* (Lhuyd's *Kyzoleth*) and *gowegneth* (Lhuyd's *Gouegneth*) certainly end in voiceless *-eth.* It would seem, therefore, that the final consonant in *bolungeth, blonogeth* (Lhuyd's *Bolonegeth* and *voleneʒeth* AB: 222) is also voiceless.

Notice further that in his transcription of Jowan Chy an Horth in AB: 251-253 Lhuyd writes *an vòr' gôth* 'the old road' and *an vòr noueth* 'the new road' with ‹th› as the final segment in both *gôth,* lenited form of *coth* 'old', and *noueth* 'new.' There is no doubt that the final consonant in *coth* 'old' is a voiceless dental fricative. Since Lhuyd seems to have taken down Jowan Chy an Horth from dictation, it is likely that he heard a voiceless final segment in the word *noueth* 'new'. This is good evidence that Cornish *noweth, nowyth* had a voiceless final.

The word *bugolath* 'shepherds' at in *Bewnans Ke* line 742 rhymes with *molath* 'curse' at line 740. Since *molath* < Latin *maledictio,* cf. Welsh *melltith,* certainly has a voiceless final segment, the rhyme suggests a voiceless final segment in *bugolath* as well.

3.3.1 *Dyweth* 'end'

That the final segment of the word 'end' was voiceless is also suggested by the rhyme of *dywet* 'end' with *whet* 'still, yet' at PC 1829-30. In PC and RD *whath* 'yet' is often spelt ‹whet›, e.g. PC 384, 397, 517, 696, 1087, 1115, 1436, etc., RD 467, 457, 1249, 1361, 1378, 1885, 2039. The word for 'end' is problematic in AB, however. In the three columns of Jowan Chy an Hordh in AB: 251-53 it occurs in various forms (ignoring initial mutation) *diwadh, diuadh, diuedh, dûadh* and *diuath.* Since the second syllable is unstressed we expect the final segment to be voiceless. This is to be seen in Lhuyd's *diuath.* Those forms in *-adh,* and *-edh* are to be ascribed to the influence of Lhuyd's native Welsh *diwedd* 'end'. Under *Terminus* 'a bound, a limit, a gole, a border, the end of a thing' at AB: 162c Lhuyd gives *Diua,* and adds: *An rect. diuath*? 'Should this correctly be *diuath*?' The answer of course is yes. *Diua* is a spoken variant of *dyweth* and agrees with the substantive in Tonkin's *gweel dua* 'to make an end' LAM 226 x 2 and with Rowe's *duah* in *An duah an dridga chaptra a Genesis* 'The end of the third chapter of Genesis' ÉCII: 185. Compare also *dho dallah* 'to begin' (‹ *dallath*) AB: 222 and *Jesus reeg dalla a boroga* 'Jesus began to preach' ÉCII: 190. As we shall see in the next section, final *-a,* where a following dental fricative has been lost, comes about when the lost segment was *-th,* not *-dh.*

3.3.2 *Trueth* 'pity', *truethek* 'piteous'

The word *trueth* 'pity, shame' is well attested in Cornish: PC 2437, 3182, RD 899, BM 345, 1608, 1992, 2008, 2168, 2937, 3065, BF: 55, 60. The derived adjective *truethek* is used adverbally at BM 2152: *me a greys truethek* 'I cried out piteously'. The related words in Breton are *truez* and *truezek,* where the final segment was originally [ð] (see, for example, HPB: 798 fn). The congener of Cornish *trueth* and Breton *truez* is not known in Welsh and Lhuyd was not led astray by Welsh in this word in Cornish. He writes *Nag ez triuath vêth dho vi* 'I do not at all pity' at AB: 244c, but he gives the adjective as *Triuadhek* AB: 48b and as *Trauedhak* at AB: 92c, 166c. This means that he writes as devoiced earlier [ð] after an unstressed syllable, but as [ð] intervocalically. This is excellent evidence that after an unstressed vowel final [ð] in Cornish was devoiced.

3.3.3 Further examples of final *-eth* > *-a* [ə]

There are further instances of unstressed *-eth* > *-a* [ə] in Cornish. A very obvious example is Tregear's *bugula devas* 'shepherds' at TH 33a contrasting with *beguleth devas* at TH 42. Another is seen in the word for 'mountain.' Lhuyd writes *meneth bîan* glossing *Collis* 'hill' at AB: 49a, 295a, literally 'small mountain'. This word is usually written *meneth* in the texts, the earliest example being *war ben vn meneth* 'to the summit of a mountain' at PA 16a and the last is probably Rowe's *hugez meneth euhall* 'huge high mountain' at ÉCII: 188. The word is also attested with the loss of the final consonant: *drys tnow, drys gun, drys mene'* 'over valley, over moor, over mountain' at BK 1161. Further examples of the loss of final *th* after an unstressed vowel include *edrege* 'regret' PA 220d, OM 538, PC 1529; *edrega* 'id.' BM 2175, 2750, BK 44 and *Gormola* 'Praise' AB: 77b. Notice further the loss of the final segment in *dues nes hagh* ***yse*** *gene* 'come near and sit with me' PC 576, where *yse* is for **eseth* 'sit!'. Similar forms are *a esa* 'will sit' BM 278 and *ty a ysa* 'you will sit' CW 47. The phonetic development was probably *-eth* [eθ] > [əθ] > [əh] > [ə] and seems to have started as early in Middle Cornish.

Kerense, kerenge, kerensa, carenga 'love' originally ended in *-th*; cf. Breton *karantez* 'love', and although the medial dental fricative does not appear in Cornish, its presence can be seen from the tetrasyllabic nature of the derived adjective *kerengeak* TH 10.

Lhuyd gives *ȝẏdreva* once (AB: 249a) with the sense 'in three days from now' i.e. the day after the day after tomorrow. It is unlikely that the word is a compound of *go* and *treveth* 'occasion'. Rather it seems as though it has been formed from *go-* 'under' + *try* 'three' + *dyth* 'day', an original **godredheth* becoming *godreveth* by dissimilation. For the semantics compare W *tradwy* 'in three days time'. At all events it seems likely that in this etymon a final unstressed *-eth, -ath* has been reduced to schwa.

The Middle Cornish word for 'ever' in the past is *bythqweth*. The second element here is *gweyth* 'time'. In the later language this becomes *biscath* Bodinar and *beska* BF: 27, 46 or *besca* LAM: 224. If final *-eth, -ath* is reduced to *-a* in this word, it seems reasonable to assume that the final *-a, -e* in *dua* 'end', *dalla* 'beginning', *bugula* 'shepherds and *mene'* 'mountain' derive from schwa + final voiceless *th* also.

3.3.4 The second person verbal ending in *-yth*

The second person singular ending of the present-future of verbs appears as *-yth* in the texts, for example, *mar mynnyth* 'if you will' PA 16d, *bethyth* 'you will be' OM 311, *ny'm gvelyth* 'you will not see me' OM 244, *mar kefyth* 'if you find' OM

1138, *a geryth* 'whom you love' OM 1278, *del leueryth* 'as you say' PC 74, etc. This unstressed desinence would have been pronounced with a voiceless final *th,* which might then be expected to reduce to **-y'* and thus become indistinguishable in some cases from the ending of the subjunctive second person singular. In consequence the second person indicative was enlarged by the addition of an enclitic *-ta,* and where possible the corresponding reduction of the preceding syllable, e.g. *a woventa se* 'do you ask' PA 80a; *mara mynta* 'if you will' CW 574; *leuerta* 'you say' PC 2017, *a ny wylta* 'don't you see?' PA 120c, *a welte* 'do you see?' PC 2925, *pandra welta* 'what do you see?' CW 1806. In other cases the desinence *-yth* was reformed as *-ys,* presumably on the basis of *os* 'you are', *gothes* 'you know.' Examples include, *ny wothvethys* 'you will not know' BK 47; *ny vethys* 'you will not be' CW 523, *na vethys* 'you will not be' CW 1178, *ny vethis* 'you will not be' CW 1183; *ny vynnys* 'you do not wish' CW 665, 823. Both *-ys* for *-yth* and *-ta* seem to be present in *Panna weal 'lesta geeal* 'What work can you do' BF: 15, where *'lesta* is for *a yllysta* 'you can'

3.3.5 The alternation *dh* ~ *th*: conclusion

Although Lhuyd seem's on occasion to have written final unstressed *-eth* as *-edh,* by analogy with *-edd* in his native Welsh, there is enough evidence to suggest that final *-dh* after an unstressed vowel was already voiceless in Middle Cornish, and that Lhuyd's writing unstressed *-edh* is unreliable. The final sequence *-eth* appears also to develop further on occasion to *-e, -a.*

Final unstressed *-eth* (› *-e, -a*) contrast with *dh* after stressed vowels in *bedh* 'be', *yn medh* 'says, said'. We thus have the same variation of stressed vowel + voiced consonant ~ unstressed vowel + voiceless consonant, which we have already noted with *g/k* and *b/p.*

CHAPTER 4
The alternation of final *f* and *v*

4.1 Confusion between ‹f› and ‹v› in Cornish orthography

Although for the most part *f* represents [f] and *v* or *u* represents [v], there is some evidence in certain texts for the use of *f* to represent [v]. This may be as a result of the influence of Old and Middle English spelling habits on Cornish orthography. In Old English *f* represents [f] in initial and final position, but [v] between vowels. The use of *f* internally for [v] is well attested in Cornish. The spelling *leverel* occurs once in OM and three times in TH; *leverell* occurs 62 times in TH; *leuerel* occurs 29 times, once in PA, seven times in OM, twelve times in PC and nine times in RD. The form *leverall* is found more than 90 times in TH, SA, BK and CW. The spelling *leferel*, however, is attested eight times, all in BM.

Notice also the following:

'he was'
ef a ve PA 156a, 215c, 233d, TH 46, SA 64, 65
eff a ve PA, TH 8a, 13a, 15a x 2, 18a, 36a, 38, 42a, 45, 46a, 49a
ef a fue PC 1606, 2186, RD 2228, 2319.

Given that *f* is used in this expression only before the diphthong *ue*, it may be that *f* is used to avoid the collocation of *v* + *u* in **ef a vue*. It must be admitted that the following do occur: *neb a vue* BM 564, *ny vue* BM 2234, *ny vue* BM 3468, 2968, *helhys vue* BM 2249, *Tregys vue* BM 2284, *megys vue* BM 4464 and *genys vvue* [sic] BM 4496.

Notice also:

ol an bys a fyth sylwys 'all the world shall be saved' OM 819
guarak a fyth settyys 'a bow shall be set' OM 1244
syr vrry a fyth lethys 'Uriah shall be killed' OM 2123
the escarn ol ketep tam gans ov bom a fyth brewys 'your bones by my blow shall be bruised every bit' OM 2743-44
rak scon why a fyth seruys 'for soon you shall be served' PC 716
y curyn a fyth syttyys auel myghtern war y pen 'his crown will be set upon his head like a king'PC 2134-35
ganso ty a fyth sauwyys 'by him you will be healed' RD 1604
ha ty a fyth rewardys 'and you will be rewarded' RD 1700
ha scon ty a fyth iuggys 'and soon you will be judged' RD 1903.

The evidence cited above suggests that Cornish scribes were aware that ‹f› could have the value of [v]. This may in part have been the result of the rearrangement after the Prosodic Shift of fortis /f̤/ and lenis /f/; see Chapter 9 below.

4.2 Final f/v after stressed syllables.

Just as final c/k represents [g] and later comes to be so written, so final *f* or *ff* after a stressed vowel indicates [v]. In the later texts final *-v* or *-ve* is written. Here are some examples:

1) 'sick'

claf OM 1337, 1568, PC 1027, 1067, 2697, RD 724, 775, 1377, 1589, 1664, 1847, BK 333, 519, 610, 1096, 2501, 2944; *claff* PA 25c, 155b, 158b, 176d, BM 1413, 1853, 3100, 3291, 3312, 3589, 3788, 4520, TH 8a; *claffe* TH 8a.

clave CW 1799, RCEV: 98; *klâv* AB: 41c; *Klâv* AB: 76a; *Denz-klâv* AB: 105b.

2) 'he, him'

ef CF 30, PA 10b, 11d, 13a, 25a, 28b, 30d, 36d, 40c, 45a, 47b, etc, OM 182, 200, 217, 223, 405, 420, 424, 433, 442, 483, etc., PC 23, 105, 184, 234, 325, 353, 360, 364, 368, 371, etc., RD 4, 24, 52, 59, 61, 122, 133, 225, 249, 273, 285, etc., BM 19, 88, 178, 440, 1694, 1903, 2784, 3989, TH 2a, 5, 8a, 23a x 2, 28a, 43, 45a, 46a; SA 59 x 6, 59a x 3, 60, 61 x 10, 61a, 62 x 2, 63, 63a x 2, 64a x 5, 65, BK 146, 237, 413, 435, 450, 536, 585, 654, 893, 909, 916, 941, etc., CW 211, 263, 321, 337, 644, 681, 710, 1541, 1639, 1652, 1694, 1791, etc.; *Ef* BK 382, 387, 429, 795, 832, 2146, 2181, 2315, 2320, 2604; *eff* PA 8d, 9d, 10d, 38c, 44d, 192c, 234b, OM 2662, BM 388, 750, 804, 870, 873, 876, 883, 989, 1007, 1021, etc., TH 1 x 2, 1a x 3, 2 x 3, 2a x 2, 3a x 3, 4 x 2, 5 x 2, 6a, 7 x 3, 7a, 8 x 7, 8a, etc., SA 60 x 2, 60a, 61, 64a, 65a; *Eff* PA 39a, BM 4385, TH 1a, 2, 2a, 8a, 10a, 11 x 3, etc.

ev RD 2017, CW 173, 818, 1408, JCH §§ 3 x 2, 13, 26, 34, 39 x 2, 40 x 2, 41, 43; *Ev* LAM: 224; AB: 230c, 246a, 246b, 247a, 247b x 3, 247c x 8, etc.; *eve* CW 209, 446, 739, 774, 777, 801, 1052, 1180, 1549, 1678, 1680, 2053, 2083, LAM: 224 x 3, 226, 228; *Eve* LAM: 224; *eave* CW 1767, 2135, BF: 39.

3) 'smith'

gof PC 1695, 2479, 2668, 2712, 2724; *goff* PA 154b, 156c, 158a; *goyff* PA 155a *Gôv diu* AB: 58a; *gove* ACB: F f 2 x 3; *Gove* ACB: P 4.

4) 'winter'

gwaf CW 366

gwave CW 1700, LAM 238; *guâv* AB: 45c; *Guâv* AB: 4c, 6a, 8c. 66c; *Gwâv* ACB: E e 4, CPR: 10; *Guâve* CPT: 11 x 2.

5) 'summer'
haf OM 31, RD 1763; *Hâf* CPR: 10
Hâv AB: 42a, ACB: E e 4; *have* LAM: 238; *Have* BF: 31.

6) 'heaven'
nef PA 23d, 47c, 58b, 72c, 93c, 213b, 214c, 226b, 244b, etc., OM 1, 7, 9, 18, 51, 105, 118, 156, 165, etc., PC 7, 79, 81, 104, 164, 226, 262, 273, 290, etc., RD 9, 136, 173, 182, 188, 227, 252, 288, 300, etc., BM 142, 154, 180, TH 59, SA 60, 62, 63, BK 1, 138, 144, 205, 238, 440, 560, 655, 793, 828, etc., CW 114, 120, 124, 149, 182, 228, 242, 301, 311, 320, etc.; *Nef* SA 62, BK 288, ACB: T 2 3 *verso*; *neff* PA 7b, 19d, 122a, BM 403, 426, 461, 465, 700, 741, 755, 1246, 1255, 1301, etc., TH 1, 2a, 3, 8a x 2, 9a, 10a, 12, 12a x 2, 16a, 20, 21, 22, 22a x 4, 23 x 2, 23a, 26, etc., SA 60 x 4, 60a x 2.
nêv ACB: E e 2 *verso* x 2; *nev* ACB: E e 2 *verso*; *nev* LAM: 238; *Nev* ACB: T 2 3 *verso*; *Neve* ACB: T 2 3 *verso*; *neve* CW 15, 23, 71, 258, BF: 52 x 4, ÉCII: 189; *neue* BF: 51, 52; *Neue* BF: 55 x 2, 56 x 2; *neave* CW 1827; *Neave* LAM: 228; *neeve* ÉCII: 184.

7) 'serpent, worm'
prif CW 1055; *preff* BM 4133, 4173.
preve CW 335, 498; *Prev* AB: 82b; *Prêv* AB: 18c, 172a; *prêv* AB: 110c; *hagar-Breeve* ÉCII: 174; *hagar-breeve* ÉCII: 175 x 2, 180 x 2.

4.3 Loss of final *v* and *f*

Final [v] is lost on occasion after stressed vowel. The most obvious example is the universal *tre* 'town; home.' Other examples include *ko* for *cov* 'memory' in *ma kothem* (‹ *ma cov dhem*) 'I remember' BF: 27; *Ma kothem* 'I remember' BF: 29 and *perkou Gwâv* (‹ *perth cov gwâv*) 'remember winter' ACB: E e 4; and *gwa* for *gwav* 'winter' in *dew whallon gwa metton* (‹ *du Halan Gwav myttyn*) 'on the morning of All Saints' day' (Wakelin: 189). The pronoun *ev* he, him' also is often reduced to *e*, particularly in low sentence stress.

After unstressed syllables, however, the final bilabial or labio-dental fricative is much more commonly lost, as can be seen from the following:

1) The superlative suffix of adjectives ends in *-e, -a* in Cornish, although the suffix corresponds to W *-af*, both deriving from an earlier **-samo-* for example, in *guella, gwelha, gwella* 'best', *dewetha* 'last' and *tekke, tecka* 'fairest.'
2) *awartha* 'above' derives from **gwartha* 'top'; cf. W *gwarthaf* 'top, summit'. No form with a final consonant is attested.
3) *clethe, cletha* 'sword' is a congener of W *cleddyf* 'sword', OIr *claideb* 'idem', but the final fricative is always absent.

4) Certain back-spellings make it clear that final ‹f› was often not pronounced. The most obvious example is perhaps *adam hag evef* 'Adam and Eve' PA 213a. Here the scribe, knowing that final ‹f› after an unstressed vowel was not pronounced, has by hypercorrection re-inserted it in the proper name *Eve, Eva.*
5) The scribe of the Creation of the World writes *ny wrugaf tha wellas* 'I did not see you' CW 1662 where by hypercorrection he has added ‹f› to the enclitic first person pronoun *-a*: *gwruga* > *gwrugaf*. He uses the same form *in ymadge dean gwregaf shapya* 'I did shape the image of man' CW 2524, where he spells it *gwregaf*. Similarly he adds ‹f› by hypercorrection to the verbal noun *bos* 'to be' + the first person enclitic *-a* in *ow bosaf* 'that I am' at CW 79, 116, 123, 318, 1264; *om bosof* CW 133; *om bosaf* CW 225.
6) *Gothaf* 'to suffer' appears as *gothe* at BM 2245 and *gotha'* at BK 2307 and as *gotha—suffer* in RCEV: 99.
7) Final *-af* occurs in the first person singular of the present future of the verb. In disyllabic and polysyllabic verbs, however, this ending frequently appears as *-a* (rarely *-e*), where the final ‹f› is not written. As somewhat random examples one might cite the following: *ny gafe* 'I find' PA 116c; *a gara* 'whom I love' RD 1319, BM 3867, BK 363, 2752, 3190; *ny gara* 'I do not love' PA 110b, BM 81, 1271, 4134; *mar calla* 'if I can' BM 426, 2281; *mara calla* 'if I can' BM 2109, BK 3216; *ny alla* 'I cannot' OM 1238, 2145, PC 2678, BM 505, 1475, 3666, 4192, TH 50a; *lauara* 'I say' CF 15, OM 1645, PC 1, 2440, RD 1311, 1928; *lavara* 'I say' BK 2750; *y leuara* 'I say' PC 59; *y fenna* 'I will' OM 17 (rhymes with *da* 'good', *tra* 'thing').
8) The first person ending of many of the prepositional pronouns ends in ‹f›, e.g. *genef, gynef* 'with me.' The final consonant is frequently omitted, however: *gene* PA 166c, OM 934, 1057, 1305, 2501, PC 218, 576, 1122, 2155, RD 2565, BM 65, 860, 1573, 1886, 2591, 2630, 3839, 4065; *gena* BM 3026, 3135, 3164, 3216, 3634, 3817, 3979, 4359, BK 75, 453, 563, 631, 797, 934, 1623, 2073, 2357, 2365, 2582, 2859, 2939, 3087; *gyne* PC 656, 1241, 1292, 1335, 1568, 2118, 2194, 2786, 2794, 2849, 3003, RD 38, 105, 112, 207, 1408, 2363, 2507, 2521. Notice also *therago* 'before me' BM 2297.

'With me' is *genevy* at BM 428, 572, 1245, 1741, 3184, 3367 and *genavy* at BM 1549, 1659, 2568. In view of the frequent occurrence of *gene* and *gena* in BM we must analyse *genevy* and *genavy* as *gene' vy* and *gena' vy* respectively, with the stress on the first syllable.

'With me' is written *geneff* at PA 64c, BM 492 and 3901; 'for me' is *ragoff* at PA 168d 'before me' is *theragoff* at BM 1849. Tregear writes *caraff* 'I love' at TH 43. We can assume, that ‹ff› is written on occasion because the scribe knew that final§ ‹f› was often dropped and he was anxious to maintain its pronunciation in these cases and in consequences doubled the letter.

4.4 The value of final ‹f› after an unstressed vowel

It is clear from 4.3 that final *f* is very frequently lost after an unstressed vowel. In this respect *-ef, -af* > *-e, -a* [ə] is comparable with the similar process we noticed above at 3.3 and 3.3.3. In the present case the development was probably [ev] or [av] > [əf] > [əh] > [ə]. The final segments in *tekka* 'fairest', *gallaf* 'I can' and *genef* 'with me', for example, were probably voiced before the Middle Cornish period. As a result of Prosodic Shift, however, voiced [v] was devoiced to [f] in unstressed position, and tended thereafter to [h] > ø. The final segment in the superlative suffix is universally lost in Cornish. The suffix was in origin **-samo-* and the historic *-s-* in the suffix was lenited to *-h-*, as can still be seen, for example, in *gwelha* 'best' PA 115b, BK 865, 883, 1055, *guelha* 'best' PC 3012, BK 1295, 2401, BF: 17. It is very likely that the presence of [h < s] at the onset of the suffix led by to the loss of its final segment [v] > [f] > [h] > ø, *gwelhaf* being simplified to *gwelha*. After all an unstressed syllable [həf] becoming [həh] would have been unlikely to survive intact. The same phenomenon probaly explains the absence of **gwarthaf, *awarthaf*, where the *rth* itself probably represented [r̥].

4.5 Final ‹v› after an unstressed vowel

Nowhere in traditional Cornish do we find ‹v› written after an unstressed vowel. The only examples of final ‹v› after an unstressed vowel are to be found in Lhuyd's *Archæologia Britannica* (AB) and in his lament for William III published by Pryce in ACB: G g 3 *verso* - G g 4 *verso* (see also LAM: 232-35). The following are some instances I have been able to find: *me a uelav* 'I see' (un-Cornish syntax!) AB: 246c; *Pernav* and *Mî a bernav* 'I will buy' (un-Cornish syntax!) AB: 247a; *Bedhav* 'I will be' AB: 245c; *Mennav* 'I will' AB: 246b; *Me a urontiav* 'I will warrant' (un-Cornish syntax!) AB: 242a; *Kemerav* 'I will take', *Ny gemerav* AB: 230c; *Guerhav* 'I will sell' AB: 246c; *ni olav*'I shall not weep' ACB: G g 4; *uarnav* 'on me'AB: 222 x 4, 224; *orthiv* 'to me' AB: 224b; *Dredhev* 'through me' AB: 244b; *A hanav* 'from me' AB: 244b. **Tanov* 'Under me' AB: 244b; *A yuhav* 'above me' AB: 224b; *genev* 'with me' AB: 223, 244b; *genniv* 'with me' ACB: G g 4; *ragov* 'for me' AB: 222. Apart from Lhuyd, there appear to be no examples of unstressed vowel + *v* anywhere in Cornish. It is reasonable to assume that Lhuyd's use of final ‹v› after unstressed syllables was suggested by his native Welsh. He writes Cornish *Bedhav* 'I will be', because Welsh has *byddaf* 'I will be' with a final [v]. Similarly he writes *genev, genniv* 'with me' by analogy with Welsh *gennyf* 'with me' with final [v], and *uarnav* 'upon me' by analogy with Welsh *arnaf* 'upon me' also with final [v].

4.6 Confusion of final unstressed *f* and *th*

Because both final unstressed *th* and *f* have a tendency to be reduced to [h] or ø, there is some confusion among items ending in either.

Mene' the reduced form of *meneth* 'mountain' is attested at BK 1161. *Clethe, cletha* 'sword' (e.g. OM 331, 1305, 1363, BM 1812, TH 25, 55a, BK 1771, 2231, CW 965) is the reduced form of **clethef*, which is not attested. The plural of *meneth, mene'* is *menyȝyow* PA 170a, *menythyow* PC 108, BK 2314 or *mynythyow* PC 2652, where the intervocalic segment is [ð]. By analogy with *menythyow* the plural of *cletha* is *cleȝyȝyow* PA 74b, *clethythyow* BK 2025, CW 325 or *clythythyow* PC 608, 1172, with intervocalic [ð].

The word *hanaf* 'drinking cup' is attested at OCV 875. The word is apparently of Germanic origin and appears in Breton as *hanaf* 'coupe'. The word occurs in TH as *haneth* in *gas an haneth ma a virnans the vos thewortha ve* 'let this cup of death pass from me.' Here *th* has been substituted for original *f*.

The Old Cornish word for 'autumn' is *kyniaf* OCV 463. This is etymologically identical with W *cynhaeaf* 'harvest' and is a compound of *kyn-* 'before' and the root seen in W *gaeaf* 'winter', Cornish *gwaf* 'winter'. A later form of the same word, with pre-occluded medial *n*, is quoted by Lhuyd as †*kidniadh* AB: 44b, †*kyniav* AB: 44b and *Kidniath* AB: 90a. Lhuyd's †*kidniadh* looks suspicious, since the obelus implies that the word is Old Cornish, but the pre-occluded *n* makes this impossible. Lhuyd's †*kyniav* is simply a respelling by Lhuyd of *kyniaf* in OCV with final *v* assumed by Lhuyd by analogy with W *cynhaeaf*. If Lhuyd's *Kidniath* is indeed genuine, it is another example of the confusion of final *f* and *th*, the forms in question being **kydnyaf* and *kidniath*.

4.7 The first person singular of prepositional pronouns in *-f*

When unstressed *f* was lost from the first person singular of prepositional pronouns, the form was recharacterized by the addition of the enclitic pronoun *vy*. This accounts for the following forms:

> *genevy* (‹ *gene'* + *vy*) BM 428, 572, 1245, 1741, 3184, 3367; *genavy* BM 1549, 1659, 2568; *ortha vee* CW 193 *ortha vy* CW 214; *orthaf vy* (for ?**ortha vy*) CW 232; *orthaf ve* (for ?**ortha ve*) CW 1429; *worthaf ve* (for ?**wortha ve*) CW 1619; *orthave* BK 1070, 1217; *thewortha ve* TH 22a.

Another way of recharacterizing the first singular of prepositional pronouns was to add *-ma* to the exposed vowel after the loss of *f*. The first example is probably *genama* 'with me' (‹ *gena'*+*ma*) PA 193d.

4.8 'Ale, beer' in Cornish

The word for 'beer, ale' is attested twice in OCV: *coruf* 858 and *coref* 861, both forms written with an apparently voiceless final segment. These Lhuyd respells from OCV as †*koruv* AB: 179c and †*korev* AB: 47b, 291b respectively, clearly believing that the final ‹f› in OCV represented [v]. In this he seems to have been led astray by the early Welsh spellings *cwrwf, cwrf* 'beer' where ‹f› represents a voiced [v]. In later Cornish the word tends to lose the second syllable, e.g. *Ha why el evah cor gwella* 'And you can drink best beer' ACB: F f 3; and cf. Lhuyd's *kor guelha* AB: 47b. In *Beunans Meriasek*, however, we read: *corff bo gvyn a cafen vy dour ny effsen eredy* 'were I to get beer or wine, I wouldn't drink water indeed' BM 661-2. Here the word for 'beer' is spelt ‹corff›, which is also the way the word for 'body' is spelt in the text, e.g. BM 523, 711, 1153, 1279, 1611, etc. There can be no doubt that *corff* 'body' in BM ends with a voiceless segment (cf. Welsh *corff* 'body', Breton *korf* 'body'). It seems reasonable, therefore, to assume that *corff* 'ale' at BM 661 also ends with a voiceless [f]. One must conjecture either that the unstressed vowel has been lost, but the final voiceless segment has remained, or more probably that the form *corff* represents a disyllable in which the unstressed second syllable is so strongly *r*-coloured that *corff* is considered an adequate spelling, where *r* represents a vocalized [r]. The word *corff* here, however, must be scanned as a monosyllable. At all events the spelling *corff* 'ale' in BM implies that the final segment of the word was voiceless and in this respect is the expected reflex of Old Cornish *coruf, coref*. The syllabic status of an anaptyctic vowel between *r* and the following consonant can incidentally be seen in *guask the vaw a'n scouoron* 'strike your servant on the ear' PC 2286, where *scofarn* 'ear' is spelt *scouoron* and must be scanned as a trisyllable.

4.9 The word for 'olive' in Cornish

The Middle English word *olive, oleve* 'olive' was borrowed from Norman French. Thence it was borrowed into Cornish. In English the ‹v› represents a voiced fricative. In Cornish, however, the final segment is always written as though voiceless: *meneth olyff* 'Mount of Olives' PA 53a; *branch olyf* 'a branch of olive' OM 1122; *branchys olyf* 'branches of olive' PC 244; *branche olyf* 'branch of olive' CW 2462. Here again the Cornish rule is seen to operate. Although the final segment is voiced in English, in Cornish, because it occurs in absolute final position after an unstressed vowel, it is voiceless.

4.10 'Caleb' in Cornish

Caleb is mentioned several times in the Old Testament, most notably in the book of Joshua. The name in Cornish is of interest. In *Origo Mundi* God the Father declares to Moses:

nyns a den vyth bynytha
a'n keth re na the'n tyr sans
marnas ***calef*** *ha iosue*
rag y the vynnas gorthye
fals duwow erbyn cregyans

'No one of those same men
shall ever go to the Holy Land
except Caleb and Joshua,
because they wished to worship
false gods contrary to the faith'
OM 1878-82

In the Latin of the Vulgate the name is *Caleb*, and in the Greek of the Septuagint *Khaleb*. Cornish appears to use a spoken form in which the final *-b-* has become a fricative. Moreover because the final segment occurs after an unstressed vowel it is devoiced. The development appears to have been *Caleb* > **Calev* > *Calef*. This is perhaps similar to Old Cornish *coref, coruf* 'ale' < **kormi-*.

4.11 The forms *sewenaffa, genaffa*

We have excellent evidence that in the first person of the present future of disyllabic verbs final unstressed *-af* ends in a voiceless [f]. The scribe of the *Creation of the World* writes *me a wore ny* ***sewenaffa*** *nefra yn beyse* 'I know I shall never prosper in the world' CW 1285-86. Here *sewenaffa* is the first person singular of the verb *seweny, soweny* 'to succeed, to prosper'; cf. *byth ny yllyn soweny* 'never can we prosper' BM 3336. The verbal form *sewenaf* 'I shall prosper' has been enlarged by the first person enclitic pronoun *-ve*, seen, for example, in *thewortha ve* 'from me' TH 22a. In *sewenaffa* the enclitic pronoun has been added directly to **sewenaf* with a voiceless final, and *-ve* [və] has been progressively assimilated to the preceding consonant to give *sewenaffa*. Similarly the scribe of CW writes *hanter an elath* ***genaffa*** *assentyes yth yns* 'half the angels are in agreement with me' CW 271-72. Here *genaffa* is to be understood as *genef, genaf* 'with me' augmented with the same first person singular enclitic pronoun *-ve*, which has also been progressively assimilated: *genaf ve* > *genaffa*. Neither *sewenaffa* nor *genaffa* can be explained unless the basic forms *sewenaf* and *genaf* ended in a voiceless *f*.

Overall, then, it seems that the distribution of final *f* ~ *v* after the Prosodic Shift resembles that of *k* ~ *g* and *th* ~ *dh*. Thus [f] appears after a final unstressed vowel and [v] after a stressed one.

4.12 The devoicing of final [dʒ] after an unstressed vowel

The Cornish rule that a voiced consonant is devoiced after an unstressed vowel is also apparent in borrowings from Middle English ending in unstressed *-age*. Thus ME *eritage, heritage* appears as *ertech* 'heritage, inheritance' with final [tʃ] at OM 354. Here also belong *damach* 'damage' BM 1077 and *ymach* 'image' BM 1805, 3789, *yamach* 'image' BM 3785. Tregear, however, writes *ymag* TH 1a x 2, 46a, presumably under the influence of English. *Mariage* 'marriage' appears as *maryach* at BM 332, although Tregear writes the word *mariag* TH 31, also presumably under the influence of English. Middle English *viage* 'journey, expedition' appears as *vyag* at OM 2163, as *vyadg* CW 484 and as *vyadge* CW 680, 708, 715, 918. The final segment here may have been influenced by the verb **vyagya* 'to journey', written *vaggya* CW 1335.

CHAPTER 5

The alternation of final *s* and *z*

5.1 The alternation of final *s* and *z*

We have seen in the preceding sections that in Middle and later Cornish original *g*, *dh* and *v* remained after stressed vowels, but were devoiced after unstressed ones. We thus have such oppositions as *wheg* 'sweet' but *carrek* 'rock', *bedh* ‹beth› 'will be' but *gwiryoneth* 'truth' and *gwav* 'winter' but *kynyaf* 'autumn'. One might expect to find something similar with *s* and *z*, namely *z* finally after a stressed vowel and *s* after an unstressed one. Since traditional Cornish orthography does not distinguish *z* from *s*, both being written ‹s›, it is necessary to go to the later texts, which distinguish *z* from *s*, for concrete evidence. There is some evidence that the distribution stressed vowel + [z] ~ unstressed vowel + [s] did indeed operate in Cornish. Here are some examples from texts other than anything written by Lhuyd:

‹z› after a stressed vowel

Beez 'world' BF: 12; *moze* 'to go' BF: 15; *deez* 'to you' BF: 15 x 2, 16 x 2; *droaz* 'brought' BF: 15; *looez* 'grey' BF: 25; *Teez* 'men, people' BF: 25 x 2; *gwrez* 'done' BF: 25.

‹s› [s] after an unstressed vowel

benegas 'blessed' BF: 8; *Benigas* 'blessed' BF: 9; *Cavas* 'to get' BF: 9; *davas* 'sheep' BF: 9; *Arlothas* 'Lady' BF: 11; *kibmias* 'permission' AB: 12.

This rather neat distribution of stressed vowel + final [z] ~ unstressed vowel + final [s] was, however, disturbed by the adoption into Cornish of a large number of English words, in particular plurals of nouns, ending in *-es* or *-ys*, but pronounced [əz]. Examples include: *bestes* 'animals' OM 124, 312, 1051; *bollys* 'bulls, ecclesiastical document' BM 2769, 2790; *chaynys* 'chains' PC 2060, BK 398; *cheyrys* 'chairs' PC 2329; *corbles* 'corbels' OM 2474; *dyscyplys* 'disciples' PA 52a, 55c; *erbys* 'herbs' BM; 1971; *floris*, *floures* 'flowers' PA 29d, OM 769; *formys* 'forms' PC 2329; *gystys* 'joists' PC 3067; *mowys* 'grimaces' PA 95c, 96a; *pagys* 'pages, servants' BM 3268; *paynys*, *peynys* 'pains' PA 3d, 6a, 59d, 86b, 185a; *revlys* 'rules' BM 69; *romes* 'rooms' OM 952; *scherewys* 'shrews, villains' PA 31a; *schorys* 'fits' BM 681; *skorgys* 'scourges' PC 2056; *spikys* 'spikes' PC 2140; *stockys* 'stocks' BM 3554; *templys* 'temples' PA 30c; *wagys* 'wages' BM 3285; *whyppys* 'whips' PC 2056; *yurlys* 'earls' BM 294.

This huge influx of words in Cornish that ended in unstressed [əz] meant that the distribution of final *z* ~ *s* became disrupted and [z] after unstressed vowels appeared not only in borrowings, but also in native words, e.g. *passiez* 'past' BF:

15; *trigaz* 'living' BF: 15; *creiez* 'called' BF: 15; *kothaz* 'fell' BF: 15; *whelaz* 'to seeek' BF: 15; *komeraz* 'took' BF: 15; *varginiaz* 'bargained' BF: 15; *thesguethaz* 'showed' BF: 15; *worraz* 'put (preterite)' BF: 16; *travaliaz* 'travelled' BF: 15, 16; *ragez* 'for you (singular)' BF: 16; *vettiaz* 'met' BF: 16; *guellaz* 'to see' BF: 16; *clappiez* 'spoken' BF: 25; *guthvaz* 'to know, to be able' BF: 25.

Since revived Cornish does not normally distinguish [s] from [z] in writing, both appearing as ‹s›, this question of the disruption of the historic distribution of final *s* ~ *z* is to some degree academic.

5.2 Initial *s* ~ z in Late Cornish

At 9.8 below I suggest that the appearance in Late Cornish texts of initial *v* in words like *venten* 'spring', *vor'* 'road' and *vorn* 'furnace' is the result of permanent lenition of the initial. The lenition of initial *f* to *v* was presumably well-established in the spoken anguage, but did not become apparent until the Late Cornish period, when ‹v› began to be written in initial position. It is noteworthy also that *fr-* and *fl-* do not appear to have been lenited to **vr-* and **vl*. The only counter-examples are Lhuyd's *Vrink* 'France' and *Vrinkak* 'French', which, I believe, are not authentic.

In Late Cornish one also finds ‹z› in initial position before a vowel. This does not appear to originate in permanent lenition. It appears to be much more random, and indeed one might argue that *s* and *z* in initial position were in the Late Cornish sources in free variation. I give here a sample of the variation of *s* and *z* which will indicate the apparent lack of motivation for *s* or *z* in any given context:

'Penzance'

a) *pensans* BF: 10

b) *Penzans* BF: 12; *Penzans* Crankan.

'salted, steeped in brine'

a) *dour sal* 'salt water' BF: 43; *Dower sal* 'salt water' BF: 44

b) *Zal* 'salt (adj.)' AB: 13c; *Pêsk zal* 'salt fish' AB: 143c

'to salt'

a) *Selliz* 'Salted' AB 143c; *Salles* 'salted' BF: 43; *salles* 'salted' BF: 44

b) *Dho zalla* 'to salt' AB: 243c.

'holy'

a) *Spiriz Sanz* 'Holy Spirit' BF: 56 x 2; *gwitha sanz* 'to keep holy' ACB: E e 3 *verso*.

b) *en zanz Garrack glase* 'in the holy Grey Rock' BF: 43; *han Speriz zanz* 'and the Holy Spirit' BF: 41; *Dar an Speris zance* 'by the Holy Spirit' BF: 41; *en Speres zance* 'in the Holy Spirit' BF: 41; *do gerriow zans gus*

Arleth Deu 'to the holy words of your Lord God' BF: 60; *en Speriz Zanz* ACB: E e 3.

'to sit'

a) *iggeva setha war* 'that he sits on' BF: 9; *ma setha* 'is sitting, sits' BF: 41; *E Sethas* 'he sat' BF: 56; *ha setha* 'and sits' ACB: E e 3.

b) *erra zetha* 'who sat' ÉCII: 190.

'sire, father'

a) *gus Seera ha Dama* 'your father and mother' BF: 55; *sira* 'father' AB: 114b, 296a; *Sira wydn* 'grandfather' AB: 3b; *sira uidn* 'grandfather' AB: 44b

b) *zeerah* ÉCII: 192 x 2; *da zeerah ha da Dam*a 'your father and mother' ADLD

'week'

a) *douthack sithen* 'twelve weeks' Bilbao; *tarthack sithen* 'thirteen weeks' Bilbao; *whe sithen warnig*[*ens*] 'twenty-six weeks'; *rag sythen warebar* 'for a week together' Bodinar

b) *zithan lebma* 'a week ago' LAM: 238; *Zeithan* 'week' AB: 33a, 148c; *An dzhÿrna-ma ụar zeithan* 'This day week' AB: 249a; *nessa zeithan* 'next week' AB: 250c.

'seventh'

a) *an Sithas deth* 'the seventh day' BF: 41; *an sithas deth* BF: 42; *an sithvas deth* 'the seventh day' BF: 42; *an sithas dêth* BF: 55 x 3.

b) *an zithvaz Deeth* 'the seventh day' RComm.

'English language'

a) *Sousenack* BF: 25, 29 x 3, 31; *Sowsnack* Bodinar

b) *Zouznak* AB: 23c, [4]2c

'Englishman'

a) *an Sausen* 'the English' BF: 25, 29; *an Sousen* 'the English' BF: 31; *Sousen-Curnow* 'Cornish Englishman' BF: 31.

b) *Zouz* 'Englishman' AB: [4]2c; *Pou an Zouzn* 'England' AB: [4]2c

'Sunday, Sabbath'

a) *a Suile* 'the Sabbath' BF: 41; *an Suil de Arlith deu* 'the Sabbath of thy Lord God' BF: 41

b) *waran zeell* 'on Sunday' BF: 39; *De'Zil* 'Sunday' BF: 55; *zil benigas* 'blessed Sabbath' BF: 55; *Zelio Tri* 'three Sundays' ACB: F f 2 *verso*; *an Zeele an Arleth Deew* RComm.

It is very difficult to see any system in the variation between *s* and *z* in the above cases. It seems that we must conclude that in Late Cornish initial *s* and *z* before vowels were indeed in free variation.

CHAPTER 6
The assibilation of *d*

6.1 The assibilation of final and intervocalic *d*

In the Old Cornish period the language possessed two different forms of *d*, a fortis /d͈/ and a lenis /d/. The fortis /d͈/ was probably pronounced with greater vigour than the lenis and occurred at the beginning of a word and in certain other contexts. The lenis was correspondingly pronounced with less vigour and occurred intervocalically and finally. Thus, for example, the Old Cornish word *da* 'good' would have been /d͈a:/, whereas *tat* 'father' would have been /t͈a:d/.

Middle English does not exhibit an opposition between fortis and lenis *d*. This meant that as a result of the anglicization of Cornish phonology by the Prosodic Shift the fortis /d͈/ in *da* was identified with the *d* of Middle English, whereas the final lenis in *tat* was affricated to *dz*. The affricate was then further simplified to *z*, giving Middle Cornish *tas* 'father' [tæ:z]. In the Old Cornish word *darat* 'door' (OCV 763) the final segment would have been a voiced lenis, but after the Shift it was affricated to *dz* and simplified to *z*. Because, however, it occurred after an unstressed vowel, it would have been devoiced to *s*: *['d͈arad] > *['daradz] > ['darəz] > ['darəs], written *daras* OM 349, 961, PC 1871.

In certain forms of Cornish the affricate derived from lenis *d* did not simplify to *z*; rather the second element was palatalized to [ʒ] giving [dʒ], written as ‹g› or ‹i/j›. The word *galluidoc* 'able, mighty' is cited at OCV 245. The *o* before the final *c* probably represents a fronted vowel [œ], which later unrounded to [e]. If the unrounding occurred earlier than the simplification of [dz] the ensuing mid-high vowel [e] seems to have been sufficient to palatalize the preceding affricate to [dʒ], and the ensuing Middle Cornish development was *gallogek* RD 2376. If, on the other hand, the unrounding did not occur until after the affricate [dz] had simplified to [z], palatalization did not occur and the Middle Cornish reflex was *gallosek* OM 1494, 2089, PC 165, etc. Palatalization occurs in other etyma, particularly before a high front vowel *e* or *y*, e.g. *begeth* 'baptism' alongside *beseth* and *pegy* 'to pray' alongside *pesy*.

6.2 Monosyllables with Old Cornish *-ui-*

A number of Middle Cornish monosyllables are the reflex of Old Cornish words ending in *-uit*, e.g. *buit* 'food' *cuit* 'wood', *guit* 'blood', *luit* 'grey' and **uit* 'age'. In these etyma the final [d] (written ‹t›) was assibilated and the diphthong [ui] or [oi] was simplified to a long vowel [u:] or [o:]. If the simplification occurred before the assibilation, the final segment appears in the later language as [z] (written ‹s›), e.g. *boys, bos* 'food' PA 10d, OM 366; *coys, cos* 'wood' OM 364, 2589; *goys, gos* 'blood' PA 45b, OM 1230; *loys, los* 'grey' OM 72, PC 789; *oys* 'age' PA

10a. If on the other hand the simplification occurred later than the assibilation, the high front coda of the diphthong was sufficient to palatalize final [dz] to [dʒ], and this is apparent in the later language. Examples of a palatalized final in such words include *oydge* 'age' CW 2101 and *Gûdzh, gûdzh* 'blood' AB: 10c, 52c, 120a, 231a, 297a. The difference betwen *oys* and *oydge,* for example, seems to have been a dialectal one and the palatalized forms are probably suggestive of a more westerly origin. Forms with [dʒ] seem on occasion to be phonetically unmotivated, e.g. *haage* 'seed' ÉCII: 181 alongside *has,* where there is no following high front vowel to palatalize the affricate [dz].

6.2.1

Assibilation in Cornish is found in internal and final position. In the next few sections I give some instances of assibilation, which give some idea of how common in the language is the phenomenon.

6.2.2 Monsyllables with historic final *d* > *s*

The following are some of the commoner monosyllables in which historic final *d* has been assibilated. In each case I cite one or two references from the Cornish texts and give the Old Cornish form or Welsh and Breton cognates. In the Cornish citations I ignore initial mutation.

bos 'to be' PA 2a (W *bod*)
boys, bos, 'food' PA 10d, OM 366 (*buit* OCV 878)
beys, bys 'world' PA 2b, OM 6 (W *bys,* B *bed*)
cas 'battle' RD 579 (W *cad*)
coys, cos 'wood' OM 2589, 364 (W *coed,* B *koad*)
eys 'corn' OM 1058, TH 57a (W *yd,* B *ed*)
me as glus 'I will make a paste of them' BM 2398 < **glusa* 'to stick, make paste of' (cf. *glut* 'bird-lime' OCV 364)
goys, gos 'blood' PA 45b, PC 824 (W *gwaed,* B *gwad*)
gulas, gwlas 'country' PA, 4a, TH 9a (W *gwlad*)
has 'seed (*coll.*)' OM 77; *haage* ÉCII: 181 (W *had,* B *had*)
hus 'magic' (W *hud,* B *hud*)
hys, heys 'length' PA 178a, OM 380 (W *hyd,* B *hed*)
les 'width' PA 178b (W *lled,* B *led*)
loys, los 'grey' OM 72, PC 789 (W *llwyd,* B *loued*)
mas 'good' PC 602 (W *mad,* B *mat*)
os 'thou art' PA 192a (W *wyt*)
scoys 'shield' BK 1632 (W *ysgwyd,* B *skoed*)
schus, skes 'shadow, suspicion' BK 1776 (*scod* OCV 492)
tas 'father' PA 3a (W *tad,* B *tad*)
thys 'to thee' PA 15a (B *dit*)
tus 'men' PA 27d (W *tud* 'people', B *tud* 'people').

6.2.3 Monosyllables with *r* before the vowel

We will see below that in disyllables if there is an *r* followed by a vowel before the intervocalic *-d-*, assibilation does not occur, e.g. *prydyth* 'poet' BK 2497. In monosyllables, however, if the vowel is preceded by *r*, assibilations is not blocked:

bras 'treachery, plot' RD 2334 (W *brad*)
brues, brus 'judgment' PA 259b, PC 1496 (W *brawd*)
brys 'mind' OM 8 (W *bryd*)
**fros* 'stream, tide'; appears as *frôz* AB: 42a (W *ffrwd*, B *froud*)
gures, gwrys 'done, made' PA 35c, OM 9 (B *graet*)
grueys, gurys 'crystal' BM 1288, BK 2981 (not in W, B)
ras 'grace' PA 3b (W *rhad*)
reys 'necessity' OM 648 (W *rhaid*, B *ret*)
**res* < Old Cornish *rid* 'ford' (W *rhyd*)
prys 'time' PA 61b (W *pryd*)
**tros* 'starling' < *trodzhan* singulative AB: 10b, 156b, 240c (*troet* OCV 514)
troys, tros 'foot' PA 46d, OM 262 (W *troed*, B *troad*).

The Cornish *grueys, gurys* 'crystal' is a reflex of **uritu-*, a metathesized form of Latin *uitrum* 'glass'. The unmetathesized form appears as *gweder* 'glass'; see 6.3.4 below.

6.2.4 Disyllables and polysyllables with assibilated internal *-d-* after a stressed vowel

The following are the attested disyllables and polysyllables that display intervocalic *-d-* assibilated to *-s-* [z] or *-j-* [dʒ]:

anfusyk, anfugyk 'unfortunate' PC 1424, RD 1520, (cf. W *anffodiog*)
beseth, begeth 'baptism' TH 20, 37 (W *bedydd*, B *badez*)
bohosek 'poor' OM 438; *bohodzhak* BF: 43 (*bochodoc* OCV 297)
Casak 'Cadoc' BK 1974 (W *Cadoc*)
cuthygyk 'sorrowful' PC 1423
dyscrygyk 'sceptical' RD 1369; *discrysik* TH 24 (B *diskredik*)
dywysyk 'assiduous' RD 1370 (cf. W *diwyd*)
gallosek, gallogek OM 1494, RD 2376 (*galluidoc* OCV 245)
genesek, genygek 'native' PC 2186, BM 2287 (cf. W *genedigol* 'native')
grajak 'thankful' BK 368 (‹ OC **gradoc*)
lagasek 'observant person' BM 1018; cf. *kabmlagadzhak* 'squint-eyed' AB 155b (‹ OC *-*lagadoc*)
Meryasek 'Meriasek' BM 31 (B *Meriadec*)
barthusek, marthojak 'wonderful, remarkable' RD 1177, BK 250 (MBret. *berzudek*)
peswartrosek, peswartrosak 'four-footed' TH 2, BK 1398 (cf. B *pevarzroadek*)

resek 'to run' OM 773 (W _rhedeg_, B _redek_)
tasek 'spiritual patron' BM 2852 (< OC *_tadec_).

6.2.5 Disyllables & polysyllables with assibilated final _s_ < _d_ after an unstressed vowel

bohes 'little' OM 384, BM 2431 (W _bychod_)
*_cablys_ in _deyow hablys_ 'Maundy Thursday' PA 41c (W _Cablyd_)
cafos, caffos 'to get, to find' PA 38b, PA 149d (MB _caffout_)
cales, calys 'hard' OM 1525, PA 196d (W _caled_)
cannas 'messenger' OM 1650 (W _cennad_, B _kannad_)
cleves 'illness' PA 157d (B _kleñved_)
clewas, clowes 'to hear' PA 79b, BM 3709 (W _clywed_, MB _cleuet_)
cowes, cowas 'shower' OM 1081, TH 31 (W _cawod_, B _kaouad_)
cummyas 'leave, permission' OM 376 (B _kimiad_)
kunys 'firewood' OM 1333 (W _cynnud_)
daras 'door' OM 349 (< OC _darat_)
davas 'sheep' OM 826 (W _dafad_, B _dañvad_)
degves 'tenth' OM 426 (W _degfed_, B _dekvet_)
densys, dengys 'manhood' PA 10d, BK 157 (W _dyndod_)
dewas 'drink' PA 42a (W _diod_, B _died_)
dewheles 'to return' OM 728 (W _dychwelyd_)
dewsys, dewges 'godhead' OM 2666, CW 6 (W _duwdod_)
dyllas 'clothes' PA 28c (W _dillad_, B _dilhad_)
dysquethes 'to show' OM 1746 (B _diskouezet_)
ezgiz, eskaz 'shoe' AB: 28a, 230c for MC *_eskys_ (W _esgid_)
gallos 'power, to be able' OM 1155 (B _galloud_)
goles 'bottom' OM 2443 (W _gwaelod_, B _goueled_)
gonys 'work; to work' PA 158b (W _gweinid_, B _gounid_)
golsowes 'to listen' TH 33a (not in Welsh or Breton)
gothfos 'to know' OM 822 (W _gwybod_, B _gouzout_)
gweras, gueres 'help, to help' PA 3a, OM 732 (W _gwared_ 'deliverance')
kegaz 'hemlock' AB: 16b, 28a for MC *_kegys_ (W _cegid_)
kemeres 'to take' PA 74c (W _cymryd_)
kerhes 'to fetch' BM 2795 (B _kerc'hat_)
kerthes 'to walk' OM 374 (W _cerdded_, B _kerzhed_)
lagas 'eye' OM 1109 (_lagat_ OCV 39, 40, 42)
lanwes 'full tide' OM 1430 (W _llanwed_)
logaz 'mice' AB: 19b (W _llygod_, B _logod_)
luhes 'lightning' RD 129 (W _lluched_, B _luc'hed_)
lynas 'nettles (_coll._)' BK 22296, TH 9 (B _linad_)
marhas 'market' PC 376 (B _marc'had_)
mynnas, mennas 'wish; to wish' PC 378, PA 70c (W _mynnyd_, B _mennad_)
Moddras 'Modred' BK 3295 (W _Medrod_)

mones 'to go' OM 264 (W *myned,* MB *monet*)
morraz 'thigh' AB: 52a, 59a for MC **morthos* (*morboit* for **morþoit* OCV 87)
nebes 'few; a little' OM 389, PC 495 (B *nebeut*)
olaz 'hearth' AB: 15a for MC **olas* (W *aelwyd,* B *oaled*)
palas 'to dig' OM 370 (B *palat*)
pehas 'sin' BM 1828 (W *pechod,* B *pec'hed*)
pryes 'spouse' OM 278 (W *priod,* B *pried*)
puskes 'fish (coll)' OM 43 (W *pysgod*)
pympes, pempas 'fifth' OM 41, TH 25 (W *pumed,* B *pempvet*)
seghes 'dryness, thirst' PC 2974 (W *syched,* B *sec'hed*)
sperys, sprys 'spirit' PA 3c, 222d (W *ysbryd,* B *spered*)
spethes 'briars' OM 275 (W *ysbyddad,* B *spezad*)
seythves 'seventh' OM 144 (W *seithfed,* B *seizhvet*)
tavas, taves 'tongue' OM 767, TH 23a (W *tafod,* B *teod*)
trevas 'harvest' OM 424 (B *trevad*)
trynsys, tryngys 'trinity' OM 1734, TH 12a (W *trindod,* B *treinded*)
wharfos 'to happen' OM 229 (MB *c'hoarvout*)
whefes 'sixth' OM 49 (W *chweched,* B *c'hwec'hvet*).

6.2.6 Plurals in *-es, -as*

Many plurals in Middle Cornish end in *-es* or *-ys* and these are in borrowings from Middle English. A number of plurals in *-es, -as,* however, reflect an earlier form in *-ed,* which has subsequently been assibilated. Such plurals include:

benenas, benenes 'women' PA 29a, OM 2247
blythes 'wolves' TH 19a x 2
byzîas 'fingers' AB: 54c for MC **besyas* (cf. B *bizied*)
iuinaz 'nails, hoofs' AB: 176b for MC **ewynas*
flehas, flehes 'children' OM 975, 932 (*flechet* OCV 135)
gyffras 'goats' TH 27a
kenkraz 'crabs' AB: 243a for MC **kencras* (cf. B *kranked,* W *crangod*)
myrhes 'daughters' OM 1039 (cf. B *merc'hed,* W *merched*)
pryues, prevas 'worms, insects' RD 2011, BK 419 (B *preñved,* W *pryfed*)
syllyes 'eels' OM 136
tebeles 'evil men' OM 1466.

6.2.7 Nouns ending in *-yas,* plural *-ysy, -ygy*

Old Cornish exhibited contains agent nouns in *-iat.* This final segment of this suffix is assibilated and appears in Middle Cornish as *-yas.* The Middle Cornish plural form of the suffix appears as *-ysy* or *-ygy.* Unfortunately there are few items which are attested in both Old Cornish and Middle Cornish together. Here are the Old Cornish instances:

Old Cornish nouns in *-iat*

brenniat 'assistant pilot' OCV 275
cheniat, keniat 'singer, player' OCV 115, 261
cherniat 'horn-blower' OCV 258
gouleueriat 'liar' OCV 423
guenoinriat 'poisoner' (*lit.* 'giver of poison') OCV 312
**guirleueriat* 'truthful person' (emended from *guirleuernat*) OCV421
gunithiat 'labourer' OCV 338
wurcheniat 'enchanter' (with lenited initial for **gorcheniat*) OCV 311
hebrenchiat 'leader' OCV 106 170
helhiat 'persecutor' OCV 317
oferiat 'priest' OCV 106
renniat 'carver' OCV§ 293, 845
scriuiniat 'scribe' OCV 351
seuyad 'tailor' OCV 291.

Middle Cornish nouns in *-yas*, plural *-ysy*, *-ygy*

denleythyas 'murderer' TH 32a
dysprynnyas 'redeemer' RD 844
formyas 'creator' RD 843
gwandresy pl. 'wanderers' TH 33
guarthevyas 'sovereign' BM 7, BK 1488
rewlysy pl. 'rulers' TH 24a
sewysy pl. 'successors, followers' TH 49
servygy, servysy pl. 'servants' PC 279, BM 3262
sylwyas 'saviour' PC 394, RD 856.

Although no etymon is found in both lists, it cannot be doubted that Middle Cornish *-yas* (pl. *-ysy, -ygy*) is the reflex of Old Cornish *-iat*. Notice also *mestrygy* 'masters' PC 1711, *mestrigy* BM 198 but *mestrysy* OM 2468.

6.2.8 Assibilation in verbal stems

Two verbs exhibit verbal nouns in final *y* in which the *s* in the stem is in variation with *g*:

'to believe' (cf. W *credu*, B *krediñ*)
cresy OM 233, 241, 1759, 17 61, etc.; *crysy* OM 1435, 1508, PC 2883, TH 38, 54a
cregy TH 16a, 59, SA 65a; *crygy* PC 1482, 1597, 1771, 2963, etc.

'to pray' (cf. B *pediñ*)
pesy PA 53c, 54d, BM 404; *pysy* OM 1607, 2140, PC 37
pegy BK 133, 426, 2335; *pygy* PC 1013, 1044, 1162.

The verb 'to reap' (cf. W *medi*, B *mediñ*) is attested only with ‹g› in the stem: *medge* ACB: F f 2; *midzhi* AB: 15c, 19a. Similarly 'to continue, to tolerate' is attested with *g* in disyllabic forms: *hy a begyas* 'it continued' PA 201a; *ny bydgyaf* 'I will not endure' CW 1365, 1509, 1670.

The stem of *gasa* 'to leave, to let' rarely exhibits ‹g› in written Cornish, although the *s* by assibilation is rhotacized in the later language (see 6.4 below). Instances include *gage* 'to leave' PC 1812, *y wokyneth na age* (past subjunctive) 'that he leave not his folly' PC 1989; *gegys* 'left' BK 1844, 2305. It is also possible that 'The Gedges,' the name of a rock in Mawnan, may represent this same verbal adjective (CPNE: 103).

The long forms of *bos* exhibit both *s* and *g* forms. In the present third person singular *usy* 'is' and *vgy* are both common. I have counted 48 examples of *usy* in OM, BM and TH. There are 42 examples of *vgy* in PA, OM, PC, RD, BM, TH, SA. The high front ending in *usy* / *vgy* is presumably the reason for the so many instances of *ugy*. A form *uge, vge* with weakened final vowel is attested eight times in SA and BK; in TH *vsa* occurs four times and *mar suga* 'if…is' three times. This appears as *igge* in the later language (BF 9 x 2, 27). The plural form with -*g*- occurs in *nyns ugens* 'are not' TH 25. In the imperfect and in other persons of the present, however, variants of the long form of *bos* only rarely exhibit -*g*- rather than -*s*-. Indeed these are the only instances of intervocalic -*g*- that I can find: *del ege* OM 796; *yth ege* PC 502; *an brassa ege* RD 1095; *yth egen* 'we were' RD 2148; *nyns ega* TH 2a; *nyns egow why* TH 16a; *mars ega* TH 55; *dell egys* BK 51; *nyng egas* BK 168; *Eth egus* BK 306; *Eth egas* BK 625; *mayth egan owth umgelly* BK 2332; *an eal ega* CW 827. The forms with intervocalic -*s*- from -*d*- are sometimes rhotacized in the later language (see 6.4 below).

6.2.9 The verbal adjective in *-es, -ys*

In Cornish the verbal adjective ends in -*es* or -*ys*, which itself represents an original suffix with final -*ed*. Welsh has no verbal adjectives of this kind, but such adjectives are common in Breton where they are written with final -*et*. Here are a very few frequently found Cornish verbal adjectives with their Middle Breton equivalents:

beneges 'blessed' OM 1745: MB *beniguet*
blamys 'blamed' PA 125d: MB *blamet*
clewys 'heard' PA 8c: MB *cleuet*
cothys 'fallen' OM 1543; MB *coezet*
curunys 'crowned' PA 166b; MB *curunet*
fethys 'defeated' PA 73a: MB *fezet*
melegas 'accursed' CW 283; MB *milliguet*
prederys 'considered' BM 2485; MB *prederet*
recevys 'accepted' BK 157: MB *recevet*
scriffes 'written' TH 2: MB *scriffet.*

Since Breton, unlike Cornish, has analogically smoothed *i*-affection out of its verbal system, there are many verbal adjectives in the language which are to that extent less similar to their Cornish equivalents. Here are some examples:

genys 'born' PA 4c: MB *ganet*
kellys 'lost' PA 153d: MB *collet*
kerys 'loved' RD 1221: MB *caret*
leuerys 'said' PA 240d: MB *lauaret*
leskys 'burnt' OM 433: MB *losquet*.

The pairs quoted above are sufficient to indicate that the Cornish verbal adjective desinence *-ys, -es* derives from earlier **-it, *-et*.

6.3.1 The second person singular of prepositional pronouns
The second person singular of the prepositional pronouns exhibit final *s* from earlier *d*. This can be seen from the followng comparisons:

ahanas, ahanes 'of thee' OM 1484, PC 2415, BM 229; OM 406, BM 528 (MW *ohonat, ohanat,* MB *ac'hanoud, ac'hanod,*)
drethos, drethas 'through thee' PC 287, 205, BK 1213 (MW *trwydot;* MB *dreizoud, drezout*)
genes, gynes, genas 'with thee' CF 8, OM 450; PC 191, RD 817; PA 78b , BM 490, TH 7 (MW *genhyt, gennyt;* MB *guenet, ganet, guenit*)
thyragos 'before thee' R 1382 (cf MB *dirazout*)
thyworthys, theworthys 'from thee' OM 822, PC 2957 (W *oddi wrthyt;* MB *diouzit, diouzhit*)
orthys, worthys 'at thee, to thee' OM 570, RD 880 (MB *ouzit, ouzid;* W *wrthyt*)
ragos, ragas 'for thee' PA 123b, BM 1985, BK 133 (MW *ragot*)
warnas, warnes 'upon thee' OM 1072, RD 1965, BM 921 (MB *oarnot, varnot*).

6.3.2 Assibilation of *d* before *w*
Assibilation of *-d-* occurs between vowels (see 6.2.4). It also occurs when *d* is immediately followed by *w*. This can be seen in two items, *peswar* 'four' and **aswy* 'gap'. *Peswar* (cf. W *pedwar*, OB *petguar*) is attested, for example, at PA 190b, RD 563, TH 37a, BK 2043, and a form with [dʒ] appears as *pager* x 2 in Bodinar's letter and Lhuyd gives *padzhar* AB: 15c, 100a, 105b, 134c, etc. **Aswy* (cf. W *adwy*, OB *hadui*) is not attested in the texts, but occurs frequently in place-names, e.g. *Assawine, Assa Govranckowe, Aja-Bullock, Adjawinjack, Adgewella,* etc.(CPNE: 12-3). It is apparent that the *w* following *d* in these two etyma was weak and is lost in **Assa-, Aja-* in toponyms and in the palatalized forms of *peswar*, i.e. *pager, padzhar*. Since *w* in this position was so weak that it was lost, it is perhaps not astonishing that the cluster *-dw-* underwent assibilation.

6.3.3 Assibilation of *d* prevented before *r*

Already in the Old Cornish period it seems that immediately before *r* lenis /d/ was strengthened to /d͈/. When, therefore as a result of the Middle Cornish Shift, /d/ was assibilated, in the consonant cluster *dr* the first element was not assibilated but fell together with unassibilated /d/. Thus, for example, *ladra* 'to steal' was already *['lad͈ra]. This developed in Middle Cornish as ['ladrə]. I list below further instances of unassibilated *dr* from the texts:

edrege, edrega 'remorse' PA 220d, BM 2175
edrek, eddrek 'remorse' PC 1440, RD 1160
goddros 'to threaten' PC 2408
kroddre 'to winnow' PC 882
Heddra 'October' BF: 38
hedre, hadre 'while, until' PA 33c, OM 2035, etc.
ladra, laddra 'to steal' RD 23, BM 2144
ladron, laddron 'robbers' PA 186d, BM 1047
meddra 'to aim' CW 1552
neddras 'adders' TH 29a
pedry, peddry 'to rot' PA 235b, OM 2705
poddrak 'rotten person' BF: 9
podren 'rotten person' BM 3323.

Notice also the personal name 'Modred' in BK (W *Medrawd, Medrod*). This appears in the following forms in the play: *Moddras* BK 3295, *Modres* BK 3179; *Modreth* BK 1487, 2779, 3265; *Moddreth* BK 3223, 3242; *Modret* BK 3080, 3100, 3164; *Modred* BK 3115. The second syllable of the name has clearly been influenced in instances by the Latin form *Modredus*. In *Moddras* and *Modres* the final segment has been assibilated, in all cases the medial cluster *-dr-* remains.

There are further toponyms which exhibit unassibilated *-dr-*, for example:

Bodrifty < *Bodrythkey* (1344) 'Rythgi's dwelling'
Bodriggy < **bod* + *rigo-*
Bodrugan < *Bodrygan* 'Rygan's dwelling'
Redruth < *rid* 'ford' + *rudh* 'red.'

6.3.4 Assibilation of *-d-* prevented when *r* occurs in the next syllable

Assibilation is also apparently blocked when the intervocalic *-d-* is followed by *r* after a short vowel. The most illustrative examples perhaps are *hus* 'magic' PC 2695, BM 3376 but *huder* 'magician' OM 565, RD 1831, 2004; and *esof* 'I am' PC 2512, *eson* 'we are' RD 1291, etc. but *yth eder, mayth eder* the autonomous form of the present long form of *bos* at OM 2794 and 2797.

Other examples include:

Cador 'Cador' (personal name) BK 1263, 1371
dader, dadder 'goodness' PC 1296, BM 485
gweder, gwedyr 'glass' BM 853, TH 6, 15a, 28a
gweader 'weaver' ACB: F f 4
lader 'robber' PA 38c, PC 1191
nader 'viper' OM 1756
pader 'prayer' BF: 41; *pederow* 'paters' PA 228c
pehadur 'sinner' PA 8b, TH 38a
peghadores 'sinner (*fem.*)' RD 1094
peder 'four' BK 824 (stage direction)
Peder, Pedyr 'Peter' PA 46a, PC 464
preder 'thought' TH 7a
predery 'to think' PA 139a, OM 205
puscador 'fisherman' TH 45a; *poscaders* pl. ÉCII: 191
salvador 'saviour' CW 1864
sylwador, sylwadur 'saviour' PC 304, RD 480.

It is probable that the singulars *lader* 'robber' and *nader* 'viper' have been influenced by their plurals, *ladron* and *neddras* respectively, and thus do not of necessity belong in the above list.

It is likely that already in the Old Cornish period *-d-* followed in the next unstressed syllable by *r* had already become a fortis. The short syllable following *d* was in all probability strongly *r*-coloured and this was itself sufficient for speakers to have taken the collocation of *d* + *r*-colouring as the equivalent of *dr*. We know that in Cornish that a short vowel after *r* was often metathesized to *r* + short vowel, e.g. in *perna* for *prena* 'to buy', *yntre* for *yntre* 'between, among', and *hydyr* CF 36, *hader* BK 1528 for *hedre* 'while.' These would seem to imply that short vowel + *r*-colouring was liable to be realized as *r*-colouring + short vowel. It is therefore not astonishing that *d* followed by a short vowel + *r* was understood as fortis / d͈ /, and so did not undergo assibilation in Middle Cornish.

The ability of *r* after *-d-* to prevent assibilation is probably also the explanation of the form *deveeder* 'sheep-worrier.' The proverb reads *Neb na gare y gy an gwra deveeder* ' He that loves not his dog will make him a choke-sheep' CPR: 9. I take *deveeder* to be for **devyder*, where the agent suffix has been added to the Old Cornish stem **devid-* 'sheep', seen in the plural *dewysyow* 'sheep' BM 2981. The *r* has blocked assibilation and the word appears in Late Cornish as *deveeder*

6.3.5 Assibilation of *-d-* prevented by *r* in the preceding syllable

The word *pridit* 'poet' is attested in OCV 263. It now appears in Middle Cornish as *prydyth* BK 2497. We have seen above (6.2.3) that in monosyllables *r* before the vowel does not prevent assibilation. In the disyllable *pridit* > *prydyth*, however, it would seem that the originally half-long vowel as it shortened following the Prosodic Shift was sufficiently close to the intervocalic *-d-* as to strengthen it and thus cause it to fall together with fortis /d͈/ > unassibilated *d*.

6.3.6 Assibilation of *-d-* prevented by *l* in the adjacent syllable

There is, as we have seen in 6.3.4, good evidence that *r* immediately following *d* + short vowel was enough to ensure that the *d* was strengthened to a fortis /d͈/ and did not in consequence assibilate. There is some evidence that a following *l* may have had the same strengthening effect:

Nadelik 'Christmas' ACB: F f 4, AB: 97a; *Nedelik* AB: 17a; *Nedelack* CPR: 11
padal 'pan' BK 1132
scudel 'dish' PA 43c.

Lhuyd also cites the word *padal* at AB: 15b, 241a, 243b, but it is not certain that these are not simply taken from *padelhoern* 'frying dish' OCV 899.

6.3.7 Assibilation prevented by *ow* in the adjacent syllable

We have seen at 6.3.2 above that *w* in the cluster *dw* is not sufficient to prevent assibilation. It does appear however that when *-ow* occurs after intervocalic *-d-* the *-d-* is strengthened to /d͈/ and is not assibilated in Middle Cornish. It would seem that the sonority of the final portion of the adjectival and nominal ending *-adow* was sufficient in the Old Cornish period to strengthen the intervocalic *-d-* to /d͈/. We thus find:

arghadow arhadow 'command' PA 247d, OM 997, PC 185, BK 403
caradow, caradov 'beloved' PA 45d, 59b, OM 721, BM 1803
casadow 'detestable, vile' PA 159a, OM 892, PC 995
defennadow 'prohibition' OM 238
dythwadow, dythewadow 'promise' OM 1624, 1871
ewnadow, unadow 'longing, desire' BM 30, BK 574, 628, 730, 1719
hep falladow, heb falladow 'without fail' OM 240, PC 465, RD 654, BM 12, BK 114
gorhemmynnadow, gorhemynnadow 'command' OM 481, 636, PC 158
peiadow, peiadov, pyiadow 'prayer' PC 24, 2651, BM 132, 2189, 3624, SA 62
plegadow, plygadow 'inclination; agreeable' OM 1008, 2115, BM 14, BK 652, CW 735.

We do find words ending in *-asow*, but these are plurals of monosyllables and dissyllables ending in ‹s› from assibilated *d*. Such plurals include:

canhasow, canhasawe 'messengers' BK 1892, CW 29
gwlasow 'countries' BM 16, TH 25a
lagasow, lagagow 'eyes' TH 3a, ÉCII: 177
rasov 'graces' BM 3916
tasow 'fathers' SA 59a, BK 2819.

These are all plurals of nouns in 6.2.2 and 6.2.3. The plural has been formed on the basis of the singular with assibilated final *s* < *d*. They do not therefore belong with the items listed above in *-adow*.

6.3.8 *Redya* 'to read' and *preggyov* 'meals'

The words *redior* 'reader' and *rediores* 'female reader' are cited in OCV 117 and 118 respectively. It is likely therefore that the verb *redya* 'to read' has been in Cornish since the Old Cornish period also. The question arises why the medial *-d-* in *redya* is not assibilated. It is suggested at 11.5 below that the yod [j] of the verbal suffix *-ya* and the plural suffixes *-yon, -yow* were able to strengthen lenis /n/ > /n͈/ in such items as *bargidnia* 'to bargain'(cf. *varginiaz* BF: 15), *ampydnyan* 'brains' (cf. *empynyon* PC 2120) and *blethydnyow* 'years' (cf. *blethynnyov* BM 3472). It seems likely therefore that the yod of the suffix *-ya* in *redya* strengthened the medial /d/ to /d͈/, which was then able to resist assibilation.

The form *preggyov* 'meals' at BM 1972 is the plural of *prys* 'time, meal' (cf. W *pryd*, B *pred*). The plural is based on the singular, possibly on an unattested variant **pryg*. Since the plural is based on the singular, absence of assibilation before the plural suffix *-yov* is not to be expected.

6.4 Rhotacization of assibilated *-d-* to *-r-*

Between vowels [z] written ‹s› is in some cases rhotacized to *r*. The only apparent examples involve long forms of *bos* 'to be', and parts of *gasa* 'to leave, to let'.

1) some examples of rhotacized variants of the long forms of *bos* 'to be':
rag neg eran cregy 'for we do not believe' SA 59
Neg eran ny ow kemeras hemma 'we do not accept this' SA 63a
Theram Ry do why an Bele ma 'I give you this ball' BF: 12
thera Trigaz en St Levan 'there lived in St Levan' BF: 15
Thera vi ybma medh Dzhûan 'I am here, said John' BF: 19
'th erama pedeere 'I think' BF: 27
rag theram en Noath 'for I am naked' ÉCII: 178
erra zetha 'who were sitting' ÉCII: 190 x 2
Thera moy Gembrack peath rig ea gweele 'What he did was more Welsh' LAM: 238
Thera vee dean boadjack an poscas 'I am a poor fisherman' Bodinar.

2) some rhotacized variants of *gasa* 'to leave, to let'
rag mar pethans gerys the vois 'for if they are allowed to go free' TH 25a
Komeer weeth na reo gara an vorr goeth 'Take care that you do not leave the old road' BF: 15
Garres ew ni 'We are left' BF: 59
gero ni guil dean en avain ni 'let us make man in our own image' BF: 52
Nena an Jowle en garaz E 'Then the Devil left him' ÉCII: 189
Ha garah Nazareth, E theath ha tregaz en Capernahum 'And leaving Nazareth he came and dwelt in Capernaum' ÉCII: 189
an Gee arass go rôza 'they left their nets' ÉCII: 191
an Gye thosympyas a garaz an goral 'they immediately left the boat' ÉCII: 192
Gwell gerres, Vel kommeres 'Better left than taken' ACB: F f 3.

There is no evidence that [z] from original *s* was ever rhotacized in Cornish. Intervocalic *-s-* occurs in the following words, for example, *asow* 'ribs' PA 218d (cf. W *asen* 'rib'); *asen* 'ass' PA 27c (cf. W *asyn* 'ass'); *besow, bezau* 'ring' BK 3308, AB: 43a (cf. B *bizoù*); *fosow* 'walls' OM 2320 (cf. W *ffosydd* 'trenches'); *kezzar* 'hail, hailstones' AB: 30b, 64a, 250b for MC **keser* (cf. B *kazarc'h*, W *cesair*); *losow* 'herbs' OM 28 (cf. W *llysau* 'herbs'). None of those exhibits rhotacization. It would seem therefore, that acoustically [z] < /d/ was different from [z] < intervocalic /s/ and that only the former was susceptible of being rhotacized. We have, however, no way of determining what exactly was the phonetic status of either sibilant.

CHAPTER 7

The assibilation of *-nt-* and *-lt-*

7.1 The assibilation of *nt* to *ns*.

The assibilation of *nt* had already begun at the time that OCV was written, probably about AD 1200 or perhaps slightly later. In OCV *-nt* is assibilated to *-ns* after a stressed vowel in *dans* 'tooth' *guins* 'wind', *nans* 'valley' and *pons* 'bridge'. Final *-nt* is assibilated to *ns* after an unstressed vowel in *abrans* 'eyebrow', *argans* 'silver, money' and *sceuens* 'lungs'. Internal *-nt-* is assibilated to *-ns-* in *camhinsic* 'unjust; injurious' and *eunhinsic* 'just'. *Oliphans* 'elephant' is presumably a recent loan from English and may well represent the plural form *olifaunce*. On the other hand *-nt-* remains unassibilated in *skientoc* 'wise' and *diskient* 'foolish.'

Since *skientoc* and *diskient* remain unassibilated at this period, it seems fair to assume that assibilation was still in progress. By the time the Middle Cornish texts came to be written, however, assibilation of *nt* is complete and occurs 1) in final position after a stressed vowel; 2) in final position after an unstressed vowel; and 3) internally.

1) ***ns* < *nt* after a stressed vowel**

bens 3rd plural past subj. of *bos* PA 159b, OM 1237 (MW *beynt*, MB *bent*)
bons, bowns 3rd plural pret. of *bos* PA 39c, CW 1003 (MW *buont*)
cans 'hundred' PA 227b, OM 1614 (W *cant*, B *kant*)
**cons* 'vagina' *gons* ACB: P 3 *verso*; *conze* Gwavas (cf. ME *cunte*, Old Frisian *kunte*)
dans; dyns, dens 'tooth, teeth' BK 718 (stage direction); PA 96c, PC 1218, SA 60 (W *dant, daint*, B *dant, dent*)
dons, downs 'they come' PA 97d, TH 25 (MW *doant*, MB *duont*)
ens 3rd plural imperf. of *bos* PA 33b, PC 2694 (MB *oent*)
gans 'with' PA 2d, 4b, OM 254, etc. (MB *gant*)
guyns, gwyns 'wind' PA 212a. PC 1215, BM 1086, BK 546 (W *gwynt*, B *gwent*)
kens, kyns 'before' PA 49b, 254b, OM 245, 2294 (W *cynt*, B *kent*)
mens, myns 'quantity, size' PA 40b, OM 69, 1592, PC 590 (W *maint*, B *ment*)
nans 'valley' in *war nans, yn nans* 'down' PA 205b, OM 165, BK 771 (W *nant* 'brook')
pons 'bridge' CF 20, OM 2804, 2811 (W *pont*, B *pont*)
sans, sens 'holy; saint, saints' PA 1a, OM 1878, BM 1876; RD 461, 2288, BM 399, BK 2881 (W *sant, saint*, B *sant, sent*)
whans 'desire' PA 1b, OM 91, PC 1092, RD 1330 (W *chwant*, B *c'hoant*)

yns 'they are' 3rd plural pres. of *bos* OM 761, 1691, RD 656 (MW *ynt*, MB *int*).

Sant 'banquet' is a recent borrowing from OE *sand* 'dish of food' and is probably not relevant here.

2) *nt* > *ns* after an unstressed vowel

bewnans, bevnans 'life' PA 12a, OM 1886
descans, dyscans 'learning, education' BM 524, TH 17a
dysquythyans, dysquythyens 'demonstration' OM 147, 1733
gorthyans 'worship' OM 85, PC 169
lafuryans 'labour' BM 480
mernans, myrnans 'death' PA 98d, OM 577, TH 4, BK 2807
skyans, skyens, skeans. 'knowledge' PA 1c, OM 82, 167, BM 213, TH 44a, CW 453 (B *skiant*)
trystans, trystyns 'sorrow' PA 222c, 53b, PC 731.

Nouns in the above list in *-yans* are similar in formation to Welsh nouns in *-iant*, e.g. *diwydiant* 'industry', *gogoniant* 'glory', *meddiant* 'authority', etc. Notice further that the 3rd person plural ending of dissyllabic and polysyllabic verbs in all tenses originally contained -**-ant*, -**-ent* or **-ont* and that the final segment was assibilated in them all. We may therefore compare, for example, *bethons* 'they will be' OM 342, 1515 (cf. MB *bezont*); *lavarsons, lauarsons* 'they said' PA 98c, 154d (cf. MB *leuersont*); *gyllens* 'they could' PA 243d, TH 37 (cf. MB *gallent, gellent*).

3) *-nt-* > *-ns-* internally

agensow, agynsow 'recently' OM 796, RD 896, 911 (B *agentaou*)
densys, dengys 'manhood' PA 10d, BK 157 (W *dyndod*)
gansa 'with them' PA 76c, PC 1431, BM 3528 (B *ganto, gante*)
ganso 'with him' CF 37, PA 7c, OM 185, etc. (B *gantañ*)
gensy 'with her' CF 23, PA 161c, BM 304 (B *ganti*)
kerense, kerensa, kerenge, carenga 'love' PA 146b, 167d, OM 1207, RD 471, TH 20a (B *karantez*)
pensevyk, pensevike, pensevicke 'prince' BM 489, SA 60a, CW 120 (*pendeuig* OCV 169)
planse, plansa 'to plant' OM 1892, 1946, TH 40 (B *plantañ*)
plynsys, plyngys 'planted' OM 2032, 2092, 2657, TH 6, 32 (B *plantet*)
skyansek 'wise, intelligent' BM 377 (B *skiantek*)
trynsys, tryngys 'trinity' OM 1734, TH 12a (W *trindod*, B *treinded*).

Historically *-nt-* in 3) above was voiceless, but after assibilation it seems that the *n* voiced the following sibilant. Such voicing can be seen in spellings like *gonȝa* 'with him' CW 324, 1583, *gonz eve* 'with him' ÉCII: 194 and *Karenza* 'love' x 3 ACB: E e 4 *verso*.

It is likely that Old Cornish had two varieties of *t*, a fortis /t͈/ and a lenis /t/. The fortis occurred initially and the lenis internally and finally after *n* and *l*. English speakers had no such opposition as /t͈/ ~ /t/ in their speech; as a result with the operation of the Prosodic Shift the opposition /t͈/ ~ /t/ was replaced by /t/ ~ /ts/. This meant that earlier *nt* and *lt* were replaced by *nts* > *ns* and *lts* > *ls* respectively. For the development *lt* > *ls* see 7.3 below).

7.2 Obstacles to the assibilation of *-nt-*

As with *-d-* however, it appears that *r* in the syllable following *-nt-* had already strengthened /t/ > /t͈/, and as a result the assibilation of *nt* > *ns* did not occur. This can be seen from the following etyma:

hanter 'half' PA 76c, PC 1401, 1741, BM 1687 (B *hanter*)
ynter 'between, among' PA 172a, BM 29, CW 1708 (B *etre*)
kenter 'nail' PA 154d, PC 2676 (B *kentr* 'éperon')
ownter, ounter, ountr 'uncle' BK 1490, 2764, 2786, AB: 44b, 114c (cf. B *eontr* 'oncle')
pronter 'priest' BM 522, TH 42a, SA 62 (*prounder* OCV 107)
terlentry 'to shine' CW 129, 223 < **lenter* (cf. B *lintr* 'éclatant').

It also seems that *l* in the following syllable had the effect of strengthening /t/ > /t͈/ and thus preventing the assibilation of *nt*. This is apparent from the following words:

antell 'snare, temptation' PA 19, *antel* ACB: E e 1 *verso*, (plural) *antylly* TH 5a (cf. B *antell* 'piège').
kantyll 'candle' TH 17a, *gantyll* TH 17a (*cantuil* OCV 782; cf. B *kantol*)
kuntel, kuntle 'to collect, to gather' BM 1508, 1515, ACB: F f 3 (cf. *cuntullet* 'congregation' OCV 185)
skentyll, skyntyll, skyantal 'wise, clever' PA 8a, 216a, BK 322 (B *skiantel* 'raisonnable')
skentoleth, skyentoleth, skyentolath 'knowledge, wisdom' BM 157, 1774, BK 1940.

With *skentyll* and *skyentoleth, skentoleth* compare *skyans* where there is no following *l* and the final *-nt* is assibilated. The form *sansoleth* 'holiness' BM 137, *sansolath* BK 1538, 1938 seems anomalous in this context, since the *l* of the suffix has not apparently prevented assibilation in the root. We must assume that the word did not emerge until the Middle Cornish period and that the abstract suffix *-oleth, -olath* was attached to the root *sans* 'holy', which had already assibilated.

It also seems that a following *n* strengthened lenis /t/ to fortis /t͈/ in the Old Cornish period and thus prevented the assibilation of *nt*. This can be seen from the following two etyma:

fenten, fentan, fynten, fyntan 'spring, well' PA 224d, OM 771, PC 650, BM 1005, TH 11, 22, BK 786, 798, 799, 818 (*funten* OCV 737; cf. B *feunteun*)
guainten, gwaynten 'spring (season)' CPR: 9; AB: 171c (*guaintoin* OCV 461).

7.3 The assibilation of *lt* > *ls*

The consonantal cluster *-lt* is assibilated in final position in Cornish. The assibilation had already begun by the time that OCV was written, for we find:

als 'seashore' OCV 733 (cf. W *allt* 'hillside', B *aod* 'coast')
chefals 'joint' OCV 81 < **kom+alt*
gols 'hair of the head' OCV 32 (W *gwallt*)
mols 'wether' OCV 604 (W *mollt*)
sols 'money' OCV 914 (W *swllt* 'shilling', B *saout* 'cattle').

There are several further etyma in Middle Cornish that exhibit assibilated *ls* < *lt* in final position:

guels, gwels 'grass' PA 16b, OM 712, TH 7 x 3; *gwelz* BF: 52 (W *gwellt*, B *geot*)
guyls, gwyls 'wild' PA 206c, OM 1254, BM 1145, TH 24, BK 2416 (W *gwyllt*).

Curiously it appears that the final segment in **alt, *golt, *solt, *guelt, *guylt* was a lenis /t/, and remained long enough to become an affricate [ts] immediately after the Prosodic Shift. The presence of an immediately preceding *l* did not prevent the assibilation of final *t* in these cases. Originally the final sibilant in *als, guels, guyls,* etc. was probably voiceless, being a reflex of earlier *-lt* which was certainly so. This is to be inferred from the word for 'wilderness' in *Beunans Meriasek*: *guelfos* BM 1127, 1964, 2794, 3213, 3368; *guelfoys* BM 3218, 3247, 3270; *guylfos* BM 2802, 3203, 4142; and *guylfoys* BM 1132, 3158. *Guelfos, guylfos* derives from **guilt* 'wild' + **bod* 'dwelling-place.' Since the second element is always written with ‹f›, it would seem that the voiceless final segment in **guilt* devoiced the initial **vod,* the lenition product of **bod* > *bos,* before itself being lost in the cluster *-ltf-* > *-lf-*.

Final assibilated *-ls* appears to have voiced, as can be seen from such spelling as *Aulz* 'coast' BF: 25.

Intervocalically assibilated *-lt-* could also palatalize as well as voice to give [ldʒ]. This can be seen from the rock name *Iliswilgig* < **enys welgek* 'grassy island' (Scilly).

7.3.1 *Alter* 'altar'

The word *alter* 'altar' < Latin *altare* (cf. Breton *aoter*) is attested at OM 1170, 1174, 1177, 1186, 1191, 1289, 1322, 1328, 1386, TH 37, 54 x 2, 56, etc. One might have expected the medial cluster -*lt*- to have assibilated. It seems, however, that assibilation has been prevented by the following -*r*.

7.4 Why was assibilation blocked?

It seems that the assibilation of *d*, was blocked by the proximity of *r*, *l*, and *ow*. The assibilaton of *nt* was prevented by the proximity of *r*, *l* and *n*. The unifying feature here is that *r*, *l*, *n* are all voiced sonants and were presumably articulated with a high degree of vigour. The collocation -*ow* was by its very nature voiced and presumably also vigorously pronounced. It seems that all these various segments had the effect of smearing their strong voicing onto the adjacent lenis and thus strengthening it to the corresponding fortis. The exact phonetic reality cannot, of course, be captured, but it is unmistakeable that *gweder* 'glass', *scudel* 'dish', *kantyll* 'candle', *fenten* 'spring' and *caradow* 'beloved', etc. have not undergone assibilation in Middle Cornish, although etyma containing similar consonants or consonant clusters do exhibit assibilation other environments. In Chapters 9 and 10 we shall see that similarly strengthening environment affected the development of *f*/*v*, *g*/*k* and *b*/*p* in Middle Cornish as well.

CHAPTER 8

Palatal assibilation of initial *t*- and *d*-

8.1 *Ty* 'house' to *chy*

The assibilation of *-nt-* is discussed at 7.1 above. The original form of the word *ty* 'house' is known from place-names, e.g. *Tywardreath, Tywarnhayle, Tehidy*, etc. Already in Middle Cornish this had assibilated and palatalized: *ty* > **tsy* > *chy*.

It has been suggested that *ty* assibilated and palatalized to *chy* because it occurred so frequently after the article *an*, and that the shift *an ty* > *an chy* was comparable with the assibilation of intervocalic *-nt-*. Although this explanation is possible, it is hardly necessary, since *te, ty* 'thou, thee' appears as *che, chee* in Late Cornish and this assibilation seems independent of any preceding item. Moreover in Middle Cornish the suffixed second person pronoun was already *sy* and *gy* < earlier **dy*, again without any apparent influence from a preceding *n* (see next section).

8.2. Late Cornish *che* for *te, ty* 'thou'

In the later language the second personal pronoun *te, ty* 'thou' has both assibilated an palatalized to *che, chee*, presumbly via the stage *tsy*: *ty* > **tsy* > *chy*. Here are a few examples:

Che ne raze debre 'Thou shalt not eat' ÉCII: 174
Che ra doone tha flehas 'Thou shalt bear thy children' ÉCII: 181
Che ra debre tha Vara 'Thou shalt eat thy bread' ÉCII: 182
Ha che, Bethalem, en Pow Judah 'And thou, Bethlehem, in Judah' ÉCII: 191
Che na raze demptya tha arleth Deew 'Thou shalt not tempt thy Lord God' ÉCII: 187
Cowzow do ve che dean mor ffeer 'Speak to me, you great wise man' ACB: F f 2 *verso*
Drefen Chee tha weele hema 'Since you have done this' ÉCII: 180
Ve vedn goerah zoer treeth Chee, ha an Vennen 'I will put anger between thee and the woman' ÉCII: 180-81
Gwrêz dah, chee gwaz vâz ha leal 'Well done, though good and loyal servant' ACB: E e 4 *verso*
Chee dên krêv leb es war tyr 'Thou strong man who art upon the land' ACB: F f 4.

In Middle Welsh the second person singular suffixed pronoun is *di, dy*. In Breton the suffixed second person pronoun is *de*. The Cornish equivalent suffixed pronouns are *sy* or *gy*, and in the latter case ‹g› means [dʒ]. Here are some examples from Middle Cornish:

suffixed emphatic *sy* 'thou'

prag y whruste sy tulle 'why didst thou beguile?' OM 277-78
prag y tolste sy 'why didst thou beguile?' OM
o dethywys dy'so sy 'that was promised to thee' OM 842
fasta sy the vreder 'confirm thy brethren' RD 1163.

suffixed emphatic *gy* 'thou'

te ȝen able ota gy 'thou man, whence dost thou come?' PA 144a
thy'so gy del lauaraf 'as I tell thee' OM 1338
nynsyw aga dev pleysys genes gy 'their God is not pleased with thee' OM 1562-63
dreys pup huny pur wyr os gy sur bynyges 'above all thou art blessed indeed' PC 417-18
ota gy ow map 'art thou my son?' RD 463
rag keusel moy yn teffry worthy's gy 'to speak more to thee indeed' RD 1727-28
the arluth avelos gy 'to a lord like thee' RD 931
Pyraga na ylta gy domethy 'Why canst thou not marry?' BM 395-96
bewe pel ny elte gy 'thou canst not live long' BM 430
gene' gy rag syngy cas 'to fight alongside thee' BK 2613
tast gy part an avallow 'taste part of the apples' CW 831.

The palatalized form *gy* is much more frequently attested than *sy*. This is presumably because the high front vowel tended to palatalize the *d* as it assibilated to [dz].

Suffixed *sy* and *gy* are clearly assibilated forms from earlier **dy*. It is not astonishing therefore that the stressed independent pronoun *te, ty* has an assibilated and palatalized variant *che, chee*. The more remarkable point is perhaps that *che, chee* does not appear until the Late Cornish period. It is very likely, however, that *ty, te* was already pronounced with an assibilated and palatalized initial at a much earlier period, but was not shown in writing.

When ‹gy› occurs after a preceding [s] in the *Creation of the World*, the initial affricate appears first to devoice to [tʃ] and then to lose the initial plosive element to become [ʃ], written ‹sch›. This can be seen in the following: *y fynses sche* CW 216; *drethas sche* CW 243; *genas sche* CW 248; *worthys sche* CW 268; and *vnas sche* CW 529.

8.3 *dy* > *j* after the article

Before ‹y› [j] initial fortis /d͈/ assibilates and palatalizes after the article in the word *dyowl* 'devil' but *an jowl* 'the devil':

'devil'

deaul RD 2088, 2104, 2111, 2121, 2506; *dyowl* OM 301, BK 135; *dyawl* BK 117, 327, 921, 940, 1786; *a thyawl* BK 678; *devle* BM 2395.

'the devil'

an Jowl BK 44, 121, 346, 546, 1164, 1476, 2290, 2938; *an Jowle* CW 1003; *an iowle* CW 1642, 1768, 1818; *an jowle* ÉCII: 186, 188, 189; *than Jowle* CW 107; *an iaul* PC 1461, 2045, RD 80, 2641; *an jawl* OM 2527.

Notice also the unexpected *an dyawl* 'the devil' BK 1786.

Once established as a common form *jowl* then becomes the universal form: *par dell osta jowle wylly* 'as you are a wily devil' CW 512.

The word *ievan* (for *jevan*) 'demon' < Latin *daemon*, occurs in *an fals ievan* 'the false devil' PC 154 and *map an ievan* 'the son of the demon' PC 2282. *Jevan* < **devan* is presumably similar in origin to *an jowl*, although the palatalizing factor was a following *e* rather than *y* [j].

8.4 Internal *dy* > *gy*

It seems that lenis *d* could assibilate and palatalize internally immediately before [j]. This can be seen in a number of etyma:

'to boil'

bredion 'boiling' OCV 901 but *Dho bridzhan* 'to boil' AB: 51c
bridzhiez, brudzhiaz 'boiled, sod' ACB: L 3
'mâ'n dzhyi a rostia ha prydzhan 'they are roasting and boiling' AB: 248a.

'belief

cregyans PA 44d, OM 1882, BM 827, 1161
crygyans PC 1813, 1994, 2406, RD 954, TH 16a x 2, 19, etc.; cf. Welsh *crediad* 'act of believing'. [Notice incidentally that this word is feminine: *mar tregowhe in gregyans na* 'if you remain in that belief' CW 176; *ty hag oll an grydgyan*[s] *na* 'you and all of that belief' CW 2317; its gender has been influenced by the synonymous *fyth* 'faith'.]

'to fly, to swim'

ov nyge 'flying' OM 1023; *y a nyg* 'they fly' OM 1068; *re nygyas* 'has floated' OM 1087; *nyedge in ker* 'fly away' CW 2451; cf. B *nijal* 'to fly, to float in the air.'

The word for 'to vomit' probably belongs here. Lhuyd gives *huedzha* 'to vomit' AB: 10b, 177b. Although the Welsh and Breton cognates are *chwydu* and *c'hwedañ, c'hwediñ* respectively, it seems likely that the Cornish verb was orignially **huedye* with a verbal noun in *-ye, -ya*. This formant was necessary, since Old Cornish **huede* would have given Middle Cornish *whese*, which would have been indistinguishable from the word for 'to perspire'.

As is apparent from Cornish *nyge* and Breton *nijal*, the phenomenon of *dy* > [dʒ] was not uniquely Cornish.

CHAPTER 9

Fortis and lenis *f*

9.1 *v* alternating with *f* before *r*

We have seen above that there is good evidence that *d* when followed by *r* does not assibilate to [z] written ‹s›. It appears that something similar happens in Cornish when *v* internally is immediately followed by *r*. Consider the following alternations:

'deliver!' ~ 'to deliver'

dylyver ȝynny barabas 'deliver Barabbas to us!' PA 126b; *delyuera* 'to deliver' TH 5, 34; *delyuerys* 'delivered' TH 10, 15a, 19, 42a; *a thelyueras* 'delivered' TH 34.

delyffre 'to deliver' PA 150a; *y ȝelyffra* 'to deliver him' PA 145d; *delyffris* 'delivered' PA 144d; *a thelyffras* 'delivered' PA 150d, 213a; *ha'y thelyffre* 'and deliver him' PC 2036.

'book' ~ 'books'

levar 'book' PA 135d, TH 56a, SA 59; *lever* TH 1a, 46a, 47a x 2, SA 62a, 63a, BF: 29 x 2; *levyr* PC 1157, TH 48a, 49, 55a, 56; *liuer* BM 101; *lyuer* TH 18a, 55; *lyver* TH 6a, 42, 45a, 47a, 49a, SA 60.

leffrov BM 95; *lyffrow* PA 17a, 73c, 206b; *lyfryov* BM 1372, 1488; *lyfryow* PC 101, 138, 435, 749, 2411.

'goat' ~ 'goats'

gaver OM 125, BM 3418; *gauer* BM 1625.

gyffras TH 27a.

'breast' ~ 'two breasts'

bron PA 169d, OM 1755, PC 676, 892, 1256, BM 3054, 4564, BK 1804.

defran CW 1910.

It appears from the above distribution that *-v-* intervocalically becomes *f* when immediately followed by *r*. I assume that the development was as follows: Old Cornish had three distinct consonants, a fortis *f* /f͈/, which occurred at the beginning of a syllable and internally before *r*, a lenis *f* /f/ which occurred internally between vowels; and /v/ in borrowings from English and French. As a result of the PS this threefold distinction was reduced to two: /f͈/ ~ /f/ ~ /v/ > /f/ ~ /v/. In initial position and before *r* Old Cornish /f͈/ appears in Middle Cornish as *f*. Between vowels on the other hand it appears as *v*. Thus we find Middle Cornish *gaver* 'goat' but *gyffras* 'goats'.

Some dialects of Breton exhibit a threefold opposition between fortis /f͈/, lenis /f/ and /v/. In these dialects the lenis member is voiced but pronounced with more vigour than /v/ (for this question see Falc'hun, 32-6). I deliberately avoid making a comparison with Breton in the matter of the threefold opposition /f͈/ ~ /f/ ~ /v/ in Cornish, since it seems wise to attempt to understand the phonology Cornish as a unique system of its own, without attempting comparisons between Cornish and other, albeit related, languages. We cannot say with any certainty whether the difference in Old Cornish between /f͈/ and /f/ was one of voicing, of articulatory vigour or of position of articulation. All we can say is that Old Cornish appears to have had a threefold opposition, which as a result of the Prosodic Shift was reduced to a binary one.

9.1.1 *Kenyver, kenefra, kenifer* 'each, every'

The word *kenyver* 'each, every' contains *nyver* 'number' (cf. W *cynifer* 'so many, as many'). It is variously spelt in the Middle Cornish texts:

keneuer PA 228c, TH 32a
kenevar BK 2679
kenyver KG1
kynyuer PA 208b, OM 1029, PC 3062, RD 2055
kynyver OM 1215
kinever BF: 58
canevar SA 60.

There is also a form in which the final syllable is metathesized from *-ver* > **-vra*. This metathesis is likely to have occurred already during the Old Cornish period, with the result that the lenis *-f-* ‹v› was strengthened to /f͈/, giving a form *kenefra*. This is in all probability a dialectal variant:

kenefra bestaz 'all beasts' BF 23: 180
kenefre vorr 'every way' BF 23: 185
kenefra geer 'every word' BF 23: 186
keneffra tra 'everything' KG1 vv 21, 25, 26, 28
keneffra Ethan Skelle 'every winged bird' KG1 v 21
keneffra lazoan 'every herb' KG1 v 29
keneffra Gwethan KG1 v 29
keneffra: bestaz 'all beasts' KG1 v 30
keneffra ethan en ebbarne 'every bird in the heavens' KG1 v 30
keneffra Lozoan Glaze 'every green herb' KG1 v 30.

The form *kenefra, keneffra* arose originally by metathesis, as a result of which original lenis /f/ was strengthened to fortis /f͈/ before *r*. There is also a variant *kenifer*, which may represent a secondary metathesis from *kenefra*. In view of the stressed second syllable with *-i-*, however, one might perhaps explain *kenifer* as a contamination of *kenefra* with the more literary *kenyver*. It may also represent a variant from a dialect in which which unstressed vowel + *r* was sufficient to strengthen /f/ to /f͈/. Here are some examples::

kaniffar plew 'every parish' LAM: 226
Kanifer Bennen 'every woman' BF: 43
kanifer guethan 'every tree' BF: 53
kanifer hethen 'every bird' BF: 52, 53
kanifer lushan 'every herb' BF: 53 x 2
kanifer tra 'everything' BF: 52 x 2, 53 x 3
kenifer tra 'everything' BF: 51
Kenifer Bennen 'every woman' BF: 44
keniffer termen 'every time' BF: 9, 12
Kenifer Chey 'every house' BF: 43
Kenifer Chy 'every house' BF: 44.

As will be seen, the attestations are all in Late Cornish sources. This may simply mean that the strengthening effect of following *r* was typical of western dialects and did not therefore become apparent until the Late Cornish period, when all writings in Cornish were of necessity western.

9.2 Cornish *neffre, neffra* 'ever, never'

The Cornish word *neffre, neffra* means 'ever' or 'never' after a negative. It was borrowed from Old English *næfre* 'never', where ‹f› represents [v]. The closest consonant to this [v] in Old Cornish would have been lenis /f/. Because the word was borrowed in the Old Cornish period, however, it came into the language early enough for the shift of /f/ > /f͈/ before *r*, thus giving Middle Cornish *neffre, neffra*. Here are a few examples (since there are so many attestations, I cite only a sample):

nefre OM 295, 314, 461, 517, 545, etc., PC 731, BM 250, 374, 1643, 2319, 2593, etc.
nefra OM 726, BM 152, 309, 460, 481, 1129, etc., BK 2842, CW 43, 58, 233, 298, 424, etc.
neffre PA 17d, 21d, 73a, 104c, 148b, 148d, etc., OM 909, 1208, 1440, 1578, 1692, etc., PC 8, 144, 552, 734, 852, etc., RD 214, 321, 498, 550, 678, 695, etc., BM 2676, 2958, 4403.
neffra PA 5d, BM 56, 63, 210, 225, 656, TH 2a, 7, 11, 11a, 17a, 20 x 2, 26a, etc., SA 60a, BK 365, 791, 874, 1036, 1609, 1617, 2148, etc., CW 661, 753, 825, 910, 915, 931, 1011, etc.

It is quite apparent that in the Middle Cornish texts the word *nefra, neffra* contained a consonant cluster [fr] in which the first element was voiceless. This is the reflex of Old Cornish /f̩/ < Old English [v] strengthened immediately before *r*.

9.3 Further examples of Middle Cornish from Old Cornish lenis *f* becoming fortis *f* before *r*

1) ***defry* 'indeed'**

The word *defry* 'indeed' frequently found as a *cheville* in Middle Cornish verse. It is etymologically the same word as Welsh *difri* 'serious' and derives from the privative prefix **dy* and *bry* 'importance'. The original internal cluster *-vr-* appears in Middle Cornish as *-fr-*, *-ffr-*. (*Yn*) *pur thefry* 'very truly' and *yn teffry* are also attested. *Defry* and its variants are so common that I cite a few instances only:

a) *defry* OM 271, 299, 772, 1022, 1950, etc., BM 59, 209, 234, 333, 448, etc., BK 1983, 1117, 2099, CW 182, 899, 1104.
b) *deffry* OM 1276, 1378, 2831, PC 282, 283, 300, 592, 646, 866, etc., RD 655, 682, 746, 784, 810, 1288, 1433, 1450, etc., BM 20, 241, BK 2643, 2904, 3229, CW 293.
c) *pur thefry* OM 707, BM 1847, 2485, 4268, 405, CW 632, 1224, 1374, 1497; *pur thefrye* CW 1955; *pur theffry* OM 1264, RD 1216, BK 323, 1038, 1200, CW 1330, 1631, 1937.
d) *yn teffry* OM 1309, 1509, 1680, PC 303, 1329, 1933, 2774, RD 217, 565, 1131, 1651, 1727, 1801, 2169.

2) ***effreth, efrethek* 'crippled'**

With Cornish *effreth* compare Welsh *efrydd* 'lame, maimed' and with Cornish *effrethek* compare Welsh *efryddiog* 'maimed, crippled'. The word is probably from a proto-British form **amriyos*, a compound of the negative prefix **am-* and **riyos* 'free' (see 2.7); cf. Welsh *rhydd* 'free.'

a) *effreth* PC 399.
b) *effrethek* BM 540, 564, 684, 4520; *effreg* TH 44a x 2, 57a x 2.

3) ***keffrannak* 'participating, associated; sharer'**

In his 1938 dictionary Nance gives *kevrannek* and tells us he based the word on Welsh and Breton. The Welsh cognate is *cyfrannog* 'partaking; partaker' and the Breton is *kevrannek* 'associé'. The Cornish word has since appeared as *keffrannak* 'participating, sharing' at BK 481. It would be difficult to find better evidence that expected *-vr-* appears as *-ffr-* in Middle Cornish. For counter-examples and the explanation for them, see 9.6 below.

9.4 Examples of *vr* > *fr* in loanwords

***lyfreson* 'expenses'**

This is a borrowing from Middle English *liveresoun, livreisun*. It is attested once in Middle Cornish, where it appears as *lyfreson* RD 676. Again it seems that *-vr-* has given *-fr-* in Cornish.

***refrance, refrence* 'reverence'**

This word is borrowed from Middle English *reverence, reveraunce, reverons*. When *v* in this word is follwed immediately by *r*, the cluster appears as *-fr-* in Cornish in the following: *Saw refrens ahanogh why* 'Saving your reverence' BK 945 and *ny wrug refrance thym in beys* 'he showed me no reverence at all' CW 1682. When there is a vowel between the *v* and the *r*, the *v* remains unstrengthened, e.g. *reuerans* BM 569, *reverons* BM 3148.

9.5 'to write' in Cornish

The Cornish word for 'to write' is a reflex of British Latin *scribo*. We have seen above how in Old Cornish *pridit* 'poet', the *r* separated from *d* by a shortening vowel was sufficient to strengthen /d/ to /d͈/ and thus to prevent its assibilating. Something similar appears to have happened with the Cornish word for 'to write' (Breton *skrivañ*). It seems that the preceding *r* rendered the vowel sufficiently strongly *r*-coloured as to strengthen the intervocalic lenis /f/ to /f͈/. This latter appears in Middle Cornish universally as ‹f› or ‹ff› after a short vowel. Here are a few instances of the verbal adjective: *scryfys* 'written' PA 17a, PC 78, RD 65, TH 46a, SA 66a; *scrifys* 'written' PA 14b, 21a, 22b, PC 1157; BM *screfys* 'written' 2766; *scryffys* 'writen' OM 2646, TH 37a, 44a.

9.6 *fr* > *vr* in later Cornish

In Modern English, which begins as early as the fifteenth century, the cluster [vr] is not uncommon. It occurs in colloquial pronunciation of *several, every, beverage*, for example and also in phrases like *fields of rye, houses of rich men*, etc. It appears that Cornish gradually lost its reluctance to pronounce [vr] internally possibly influenced by the presence of [vr] in English,. At all events the later language replaced [fr] with [vr] in many cases. In many instances the shift from *-fr-* to *-vr-* is perhaps better ascribed to the operation of analogy than by imitation of English.

1) **'books'**

We have seen at 9.1 above that the singular *lever, lyver* has a plural *leffrov, lyffrow, lyfryow*. The distinct stem in the plural is replaced in the later language by adding *-ow* to the singular stem: *leverow* 'books' CW 2175, 1193, 2197; *leverowe* 'books' CW 2185; *levra coth* 'old books' BF: 48; *levar*… plur. *livrou* AB: 78c; *Levrou* AB: 242a x 6; *Levrou* AB: 242c.

Notice incidentally that the singular *ov lefer* 'my book' occurs at BM 1418, *an lefer* 'the book' at BM 1499 and *lyffer* 'book' at TH 18a. These forms could quite easily be graphemic only. It is also possible, however, that they are variants from a variety of Cornish in which unstressed vowel + *r* was sufficient to strengthen preceding /f/ > /f͈/, and thus give ‹f› or ‹ff› in Middle Cornish. With this possible development compare *keniffer* < *kenyver* at 9.1 above.

2) **'arms'**

The Cornish for 'arm of the body' is *bregh* OM 262; cf. *the vregh* 'your arm' PC 2733, BM 3631. The dual occurs in *y ȝefregh* 'his arms' PA 76a; *hay ȝeffregh* 'and his arms' PA 232a. In these two instances lenited *-vr-* appears as *-fr-*. In other texts, however, *-vr-* has been restored: ov *dyv-vregh* 'my arms' OM 688; *y thyw-vreg* 'his arms' PC 1179; *the thyv-vregh* 'your arms' PC 1189; *ow dywvregh* 'my arms' PC 3159; *ha thyw vregh* 'and his arms' RD 1265.

Notice also that alongside *defran* CW 1910, there is *devra* CW 1837, which is an error for *devran* 'two breasts, bosom'; if so, it shows that *defran* < *dywfron* had become *devran.*

3) **'ever, never'**

Although *nefra, neffra* is the form of this word during the Middle Cornish period, a form with *-vr-* for the medial *-fr-* appears in later texts: *nevra* CW 31, ÉCII: 184, AB: 101b x 2, 176c, 230c. This also appears as *nevera* CW 469, BF: 41, ACB: E e 4 *verso*, ACB: F f ; and *neverah* BF: 39.

4) **'indeed'**

Although forms with internal *-fr-* or *-ffr-* (*defry, deffry,* , etc.) are attested over 120 times in Middle Cornish, in the later language variants with medial *-ver-* occur: *purthevry* BM 1948, *pur thevrey* BM 2359; *devery* CW 136, 169, 208, 340; *deverye* CW 131; *in tevery* CW 101, 1130; *yn tevery* CW 531. This development is comparable with *neffra* > *nevra,* and is apparently absent from the earliest Middle Cornish.

5) **'to deliver'**

We have seen at 9.1 above that the verbal noun 'to deliver' is usually *delyffra* or *delyfrya* in PA and the Ordinalia, and that when inherited *v* is separated by a vowel from the following *r*, the *v* remains. Forms like *delyver* in which *v* is not strengthened to *f* because it is followed by a vowel, appear in some cases to have formed the basis for analogical forms of the verbal noun with *-vr-*. I know of only one example: *delyvrya* 'to deliver' BM 3736. The verbal adjective *delyverys* 'delivered' CW 2463 is a possible further example, since the metre requires that the word be scanned as a trisyllable and thus it must be understood as **delyvrys*.

6) **'participating'**

Attention has been drawn to *keffrannak* at BK 481. A variant with *-vr-* is also attested however: *kevrennek* TH 35; TH 51. This may simply be a variant spelling for *keverennak* TH 12a, where the *v* and *r* are separated by a vowel.

7) **'to expose, to betray'**

This word is attested with *-vr-* or *-ver-* only: *erna vons e dyskevrys* 'until they are disclosed' BK 3160; *mara qwrees ow dyskevera* 'if you betray me' CW 577; *tha theskyvra* 'to betray you' CW 578. If we had more Cornish we might perhaps find examples of an earlier **dyskeffra*.

9.6.1 'Sovereign' in Cornish

This word is attested several times in Cornish: *soueran* BM 246; *Soueregn* TH 2; *soveran* TH 4a x 2; *sefryn* OM 2189; *sofran* BK 1309; *suffran* BK 2476, 2697. The variants *soueran, soveran* ~ *sefryn, sofran, suffran* could possibly be ascribed to the phenomenon we have been describing: *-ver-* but *-ffr-*. This is a loanword from Middle English and the Middle English forms of the word include *soverain* and *suffrane*. There is therefore no need to invoke a shift *-fr-* to *-vr-* to explain Cornish *sefryn, sofran, suffran*.

9.7 Evidence of *-vl-* > *-fl-*

There is good evidence also that Old Cornish lenis /f/ is strengthened to fortis /f̤/ immediately before *l* and the cluster appears as *-fl-* in Middle Cornish.

The word *afles* occurs in *The afles a bredireth, te fals goky* 'you are entertaining your own disadvantage, you false fool' at BK 160-1. The word is not otherwise attested but is from the negative prefix *av-* and *les* 'advantage. The cluster *-vl-* appears as ‹fl›.

The Cornish cognate of Breton *divlam* 'innocent, without blame' is a compound of privative *dy-* and *blam* 'blame'. It appears as *deflam* in *yn meȝens y forth nyng es may hallo bos deflam guris* 'there is no way, they said, that she can be rendered guiltless' PA 32d.

The Cornish cognate of Welsh *diflas* 'distastful, tasteless', Breton *divlaz* 'insipid' is a compound of *dy* and *blas* 'savour, tang'. It appears in Cornish as *dyflas* 'distastefully' PC 2604 and in the phrase *mar thyfflas* 'so distastefully PC 1418. Similarly the derived verb (Welsh *diflasu* 'to disgust', Breton *divlazañ* 'to render insipid') occurs as *dyflase* 'to cause to be disgusted' PC 901.

The best attested example of *vl* > *fl* occurs in the word *aflythys* 'hardened, tough, stubborn', a compound of the negative prefix *av-* and a verbal adjective **lythys* 'softened' < * *lyth* 'soft'; cf. Welsh *llaith* 'soft, damp'. The word occurs as an adjective in *re iovyn arluth a'n beys del leueryth a vyth gurys the'n plosek guas* *aflythys* 'by Jove, lord of the world, as you say will be done to the dirty stubborn fellow' PC 449-51. It appears as a plural substantive in *powesough aflythygyon rag marow yv an voron* 'stop, you stubborn men, for the young woman is dead' OM 2745-46. In the later text CW (written 1611) the cluster *-fl-* has been replaced with *-vl-*: *cooth ew eve hag avlethis* 'he is old and stubborn' CW 1052.

9.8 Initial *f* > *v* in Late Cornish

It is noteworthy that in Late Cornish sources historic *f* is sometimes written ‹v› in initial position. Here are some examples:

***fenten* 'spring, well'**
ventan 'a well or spring' AB: 289a; *VENTON* 'a well' ACB: A a 2 *verso; the'n venton* 'to the well' ACB: F f 2c *verso; parc an venton* 'the well field' Crankan.

***foge* 'blowing-house'**
Voge toponym CPNE: 98; *Chyvogue* toponym CPNE: 98; *Whel an Voag* toponym CPNE: 98.

**fals 'sickle'*
Voulz AB: 58b, 293a

***forth* 'road, way'**
an vorr goeth 'the old road'BF: 15; *rag an vorr noueth* 'for the new road' BF: 15; *an vòr noueth* 'the new road' BF: 17; *an vòr gôth* 'the old road' BF: 17; *An vordh* 'The way' AB: 241c; *kenefre vor* 'every way' ÉCII: 185; *reb an vor* 'beside the way' ÉCII: 190; *vor arall* 'another way' ÉCII: 197.

***forn* 'furnace'**
Vorn 'An Oven' AB: 22a; *Vorn* 'Furnus…An oven, a furnace, a kiln' AB: 62b; *tzhÿi vorn* 'A bake-house' AB: 121a.

***forgh* 'fork'**
Vorh 'a fork' AB: 22a. 62b; *Vorh trivorh* 'Any tool or instrument that hath three teeth' AB: 166c

***fos* 'wall'**
a goye da vozou 'within thy walls' RC 24: 7; *Foza, Voza* [both < *Vosow*], *Vose* 'an intrenchment' ACB: O 4 *verso*.

All these etyma are feminine and in the singular after the definite article the initial consonant was lenited. Indeed Lhuyd tells us that *An vordh* is the lenited form of *fordh* 'way' after the definite article (AB: 241c). The lenition of *f* > *v* in feminines after the article may not have been universal in Cornish; but may rather have been dialectal. In this context we should not that Lhuyd gives *filh* alongside *voulz* 'sickle' 58b, 293a. He also gives *Fôs* 'wall' AB: 3a. 230c, 242c and *Fossou, Fosou* 'walls' AB: 242c; but no example with initial *v*. Similarly Pryce gives *en foarn* 'in the oven' and *an foge* 'the blowing-house' ACB: F f *verso*. Note also the plural *guz furu* 'your ways' LAM: 243. It seems nonetheless that the etyma listed above acquired permanent lenition in the singular.

The initial *f* of *feer* 'wise' (Middle Cornish *fur*) is lenited to *v* in *teeze veer* 'wise men' ÉCII 194; *an deeze feere* 'the wise men' ÉCII: 195. But notice also *an teeze feere* ÉCII: 199. Lenition of the adjective after *tus* 'men' is common in Middle Cornish, but not universal: *a dus tha* 'O good men' TH 10; *an dus tha* 'the good men' TH 25; *tus tha* 'good men' TH 25a; *why tus tha* 'you good men' TH 35 but *tus dall* 'blind men' BM 786, 804; *tus mas* 'good men' TH 27; *tus diskys* 'learned men' TH 38.

It should be noted that in Late Cornish texts initial *f* is not lenited to *v* other than as the initial consonant of a singular feminine noun or a masculine plural adjective. Among Late Cornish items beginning with *f* one can include:

foulze 'false' ÉCII: 174
tha gwelle onen feere 'to make one wise' ÉCII: 176
figgez 'figs' ÉCII: 177
ha fesias gy 'and chased them' LAM: 224
Me rig fanja 'I received' LAM: 239
tha'n fer 'to the fair' ACB: F f *verso*.

The only example I can find of *f* > *v* other than in a feminine singular noun or a masculine plural one is Borde's *Vata lew genar why?* (leg. *Vatal ew genoh why?*) 'How are you?' (Loth 1900: 262), where *Vatal* means 'How?' The more usual form of this adverb in Late Cornish, however, is *fatal, fatel, fatl*, as can be seen in the following examples:

Fatlu gan awhy? (leg. *Fatl u gana why*) 'How are you' Carew: 127
fatla eue a reeg dose 'how it came' BF: 29
perêg E gwellaz fatal o geaze gwreaze anotha 'when he saw that he had been mocked' ÉCII: 199
Fatla ello why geil? po, fatla gan a why 'How do you do? or How is it with you?' ACB: F f *verso*
Fatla gura ve agaz gorra why en dowr 'What if I lay you on the ground' ACB: F f 4 *verso*
Fatell 'How' AB: 231a
Fatla 'How' AB: 134c, 135c
fatla 'how' AB: 248c.

Lhuyd also cites forms *Pattel* and *Patla* which are not found elsewhere.

It has been suggested above that initial *v* in Late Cornish for historic *f* has come about generalizing the lenited form of the initial consonant. While Borde's *Vatal* could, in theory, be *Fatal* with lenited initial, it is difficult to see in what context the initial consonant of *Fatal* 'how?' could have been lenited.

9.9 The Cornish for 'France' and 'French'

The forms cited in 9.8 above (*venton, voge, voulz, vorn, vorr* and *vorh*) all exhibit permanent lenition of *f* before a vowel. Since all six etyma are feminine singular nouns, it is likely that the lenition first occurred first after the definite article *an*, though it would have occurred after *the* 'thy', *y* 'his' and *the* 'to' also. It has also been suggested at 9.1 and 9.7 that expected *v* does not appear in Middle Cornish before *r* or *l*, being replaced by *f* in both cases. It seems probable also that where the clusters *fr* and *fl* occurred at the beginning of a word the initial *f* remained unlenited in those places where an unprotected *f* would have undergone lenition. In which case some dialects at least of spoken Middle Cornish probably said *the vorgh* 'your fork', *y venten* 'his spring' and *the vorth aral* 'to another way'. On the other hand 'your child' would have been *the flogh* (not *the *vlogh*), 'his nose' would have been *y frigow* (not *y *vrigow*) and 'very free' would have been *por frank* (not *por *vrank*). This is presumably why words beginning in Middle Cornish with *fr* and *fl* do not appear in Late Cornish texts with initial **vr* or **vl*. Here are some examples:

Pow an Flemmen 'Flanders' LAM: 226

flo 'child' Symonds; *den na flôh* 'man or child' BF: 18; *an flô* 'the child' ÉCII: 196 x 2, 197; *gen flô* 'with the child' ACB: F f 4 *verso*; *tha flehas* 'your children' ÉCII: 181; *rag an Flehaz* 'for the children' BF: 29; *en dula a Flehaz* 'in my children's hands' BF: 31; *war an flehas* 'upon the children' BF: 41; *vor an fleaz* 'upon the children' BF: 55

fraga, rag fraga, rag fra 'why?' AB: 53a; *Rag fraga, rag fra* 'why' AB: 134a; *rag fra* 'why?' AB: 242b; *fraga...rag fra* 'why? AB 248c; *Rag fraga* 'Why?' BF: 39.

Frank 'free' ACB: E e 4 *verso*

frantik 'lunatic' ÉCII: 193

freegaw, freeg 'nose, nostrils' RCEV: 97; *Frigau* 'nose' AB: 97a, 295a; *frigo* 'nose' Symonds

Dho fría 'to fry' AB: 61b.

frîez 'freed' BF: 18.

frodin 'bridle' Symonds; *frudn* 'a bridle' ACB: O 4 *verso*.

frôth 'spitefulness' BF: 19.

An frôz 'the tide' AB: 42a.

In view of all the above forms with initial *fr-* in Late Cornish, one would expect the words for 'France', 'Frenchman' and 'French language' to begin with *fr-* also. This does indeed seem to be the case. I have collected the following examples both from Middle Cornish and Late Cornish sources:

'France'
Frynk BK 2735
Frenk BF: 29
Frink LAM: 226 x 2
Kynyphan frenk 'Walnut' [literally 'nut of France'] AB: 74a
Pokkys Frenk 'The Pox' [i.e. syphilis; literally 'the pox of France'] AB: 82a.

'Frenchman'
Francan-belgan 'Franco-Belgian' BF: 31.

'French language'
Frenkock BF: 29, 59
Frenkek AB: 222, 223.

Some toponyms exhibit initial *fr*: *Trefranck, Ponsfrancke, Adgyan Frank* and *Bosfranken*. In others *f* has been lost: *Trerank, Tranken* and *Trink* (CPNE: 100). There appear to be no examples of **Vrynk, *Vrank* or **Vrenkek* in traditional sources. The only exceptions seem to be Lhuyd's *Vrink* 'France' AB: 222 and *Vrinkak* 'French language' AB: 62c, both of which are repeated by Pryce (ACB: A a 3 *verso*). In view of the absence of any etyma from native sources beginning with *vr-*, it seems probable that Lhuyd's *Vrink* and *Vrinkak* are his own creations, based on the mistaken idea that every initial *f* in Cornish becomes *v* in the contemporary language.

CHAPTER 10

Fortis and lenis *k* and *p*

10.1 Fortis and lenis *k*

There is some evidence that Old Cornish distinguished between a fortis *k* /k͈/ and a lenis /k/. The fortis occurred in initial position and probably also in certain internal consonant clusters, *-sk-* for example. As a result of the PS the fortis was identified with English /k/ in loanwords and was written ‹c›, ‹k›, and ‹q› before [w]. Between vowels and in final position after a stressed vowel the lenis /k/ was identified with English /g/. As has been noted at 2.6 above this /g/ was usually written ‹k› in the earliest texts, but this spelling yielded to ‹g› in later sources. Thus earlier *kyk* 'flesh' gave way to *kyg*, *gwrek* 'wife' to *gwreg* and *whek* 'sweet' to *wheg*. It must be remembered that in *kyk*, *gwrek*, *whek*, etc., the spelling is deceptive. Although the final segment was written ‹k›, it was, I assume, pronounced as a lenis /k/ in Old Cornish and after the Prosodic Shift as [g].

The word *drok* 'evil' is a well-attested etymon with final [g] written ‹k› at first but later with ‹g›. It appears both as a prefixed form and as free-standing predicative adjective and noun, the latter meaning 'evil' and 'evil person'. Here are some examples from the texts:

Prefix

drok PA 192a, 202a, 1230, PC 12, 263, 991, 1125, 1128, 2018, 2247, 2727, 2782, 2902, 2913, 2975, 3066, 3075, 3089, 3097, RD 280, 512, 678, 1564, 1782, 1888, 2002, 2086, 2159, 2186, 2228, 2346, 2423, 2570, 2576, 1325, 2333, 2643, 2657, 3206, 3760, 3859

droke CW 646, 769

throk BM 2358.

drog OM 550, 2324, 2742, 3722, TH 6a, 9 x 2, 24, 24a x 2, 25 x 5, 29a, 30, 31a x 3, 32a, 40, 40a, 48, BK 117, 459, 471, 488, 756, 3278, CW 927, 1441, 1485, 1655, 1721, 1919, 2141

throg TH 24a, 28a, 42, BK 473, 1498, 2212, 3144, CW 1418

droge CW 2398.

Predicative adjective

drok PA 259b, PC 1142, 1192, 2967, RD 207, 298, 1129, 1284, 1455, 2363, BM 909.

drog OM 417, 917, BM 457, BK 27.

Substantive

drok PA 21b, 24d, 60c, 94c, 96b, 101d, 112d, 119d, 120a, 145b, 194b, 237b, OM 291, 601, 617, PC 338, 1404, 1945, 2113, 2192, 2435, 2775, RD 278, 498, 659, 1432, 1783, 1815, 1832, 1862, 1871, 1914, 2020, BM 29, 1265, 1276, 1891, 2345, 2424, 3372, 3385, 3421, 3752, 4087, 4144, 228
throk PC 2098, 2887, BM 1898, 2265
throke CW 937
druk OM 628
trok RD 1730.
drog OM 1402, 1569, TH 2a, 3a, 22 x 2, 30 x 2, 34, 46a, BK 10, 350, 524, 542, 572, 790, 1166
throg OM 1601, TH 23, 29, BK 3101, CW 1412
drug BK 599.

Derived from *drog* there is an abstract noun *drockoleth* 'evil, wickedness'. On the basis of *skentoleth* from *skentyl*, it is probable that *drockoleth* derives from an otherwise unattested adjective **drockyl*. We have noted above that a vowel + *l* strengthened lenis /d/ to /d͈/ so that it did not affricate, e.g. in *scudel* and *Nadelik*. We have also note here that the same suffix strengthens the *t* in *-nt-*, for example, in *skentyl* and thus prevents assibilation. This can be clearly seen in the contrast between *skyans* but *skentyl, skentoleth*. It seems probable therefore in the present case that the *l* in the suffixes **-yl* and *-oleth* strengthened the final segment of the root from /k/ to /k͈/, giving *drockoleth* in Middle Cornish. Here are all the instances of *drockoleth* that I have been able to find:

drocoleth PC 1864, TH 55a footnote
drockoleth TH 5, 9a
drockolleth TH 11a
drogkoleth TH 7, 8a, 42
drogkolleth TH 3, 10a
drokcoleth BM 1768
drokkuleth PC 2007
drokoleth TH 39
throckoleth TH 23.

Every one of the above spellings contains either *c, ck, gk* or *k* at end of the first syllable. This suggests that the segment was voiceless, even though it occurs between vowels. The most likely explanation is that the following *l* strengthened Old Cornish lenis /k/ to fortis /k͈/ and that this appears as [k] after the Prosodic Shift.

It is clear from the spellings of *drocoleth* that intervocalic *-k-* was part of the Middle Cornish sound system. In which case, the recent argument that *-k-* in *dukys* 'dukes' represents an innovation to the system, cannot be sustained. Indeed Middle Cornish exhibits several further examples of intervocalic *-k-* variously spelt: *fekyl cher* 'fawning demeanour' PA 65c; *menough rebekis* 'often rebuked' PA 2c; *veyll rebukis* 'vilely rebuked' PA 156a; *an spykys* 'the spikes' PA 159d; *an spikys* 'the spikes' PC 2140; *strekis* 'strokes' PA 227b; *strocosow, strokosow* 'strokes, blows' PA 173b, 174c, OM 2225; *penakyll, pynakyl* 'pinacle' PA 13c, PC 84, 88; *gans an eȝewon goky* 'by the foolish Jews' PA 238a; *tackis, tackys* 'attached' PA 179b, 189a, PC 2518, RD 1116; *forsakis* 'forsaken' BM 1941; etc.

Jago cites the dialect word *fackle* 'an acute inflammation of the foot'. Nance included this, spelt *fakel,* in his 1938 dictionary to mean 'inflammation' and 'torch'. With this latter sense compare W *ffagl* 'torch, flame' < Latin *facula* 'a little torch'. If the comparison with Welsh is valid, the Cornish dialect form *fackle* with a voiceless [k] is trustworthy, since the following *l* would have strengthened the preceding /k/ to /k͈/, which after the shift would appear as [k]. The emendation of this word to **fagel* would seem to be mistaken.

10.2 Fortis and lenis *p*

Symmetry would lead us to assume that Old Cornish had a fortis /p͈/ and a lenis /p/. The fortis would occur initially and in certain internal clusters. The lenis /p/ would appear between vowels and in final position. After the Prosodic Shift the fortis would be expected to appear as *p,* while the lenis would be written *b* internally, but as *p* finally. After stressed vowels this final *p* (representing [b]) was replaced in later texts by *b.* I say later texts but it is clear that final [b] was written as ‹b› in the earliest Middle Cornish in some words, e.g. *mab* PA 1a, 3b, 7a, 8d, 9c, 11c, 12a, 14d, etc.

We have seen that an unstressed vowel + *l* in the next syllable strengthens /d/ > /d͈/ in *scudel, Nadelik,* /nt/ > /nt͈/ in *skentyl, skentoleth,* and /k/ > /k͈/ to give *drocoleth* rather than **drogoleth.* There is some evidence after an unstressed vowel *l* strengthens intervocalic /p/ > /p͈/ so that it occurs in Middle Cornish as *p* rather than the expected *b.* This development is not well attested and may have been dialectal and sporadic only. Here are some possible examples:

> ***popel*** for ***pobel*** 'people'
> *ov popel* 'my people' OM 1416; *popel ysral* 'the people of Israel' OM 1489; *y popel* 'his people' OM 1512; *an popel* 'the people' PC 2465; *tebel popel* 'evil people' PC 3184.
>
> ***capel*** for ****cabel*** 'cable'
> *capel gorhel* 'a ship's cable' BM 467.

It is also possible that *r* after a stressed vowel strengthened a preceding /p/ to /p͈/. If so this might explain the form *opery* 'to work' BM 2613 rather than **obery*. *Oberys* 'wrought' with internal ‹b› is attested elsewhere, i.e. OM 15, 291, RD 1224. The form *aparth* in *aparth an Tas* 'In the name of the Father' BK 2768 may also belong here. Notice also *troplys* 'troubled' PC 26 which contrasts with the later form *trobles* 'troubled' CW 1460.

CHAPTER 11
Pre-occlusion

11.1 Pre-occlusion of *n*

Pre-occlusion is a phenomenon unique to Cornish among the Brythonic languages, although it does occur in Manx Gaelic. It means that when *n* or *m* follow a short stressed syllable, the sonant is preceded by a slight unexploded stop. Thus *pen* 'head' develops as *pedn,* and *cam* 'bent' as *cabm.* Although pre-occlusion is not attested in writing until the early sixteenth century, there can be no doubt that its origins are much older, and indeed that it was initially provoked by the Prosodic Shift.

Let us start with pre-occlusion of *n.* Old Cornish had a fortis /n͈/ and a lenis /n/. Whether these were distinguished by length or by position of articulation is impossible to say. /n͈/ occurred initially, e.g. in *nerth* 'strength' as a reflex of British initial *n.* It also occurred internally or finally as the reflex of earlier geminate *-nn-* or *-nd-*. Thus *pen* 'head' in Old Cornish was /pen͈/ since the final segment was originally a geminate; cf. Old Irish *cenn* 'head' (< **kwenno-*). The lenis /n/ occurred initially as a product of lenition, e.g. *y nerth* /i nerθ/ 'his strength' and as a reflex of an etymologically single *n* between vowels, e.g. *benen* 'woman'.

The opposition /n͈/ ~/ n/ was and is unknown in English. In consequence as a result of the Prosodic Shift the opposition /n͈/ ~ /n/ was replaced by /n/ ~ /^{d}n/, where the second phoneme was the Anglophone's attempt to imitate a long /n͈/, i.e. by reshaping the fortis as his *n* preceded by a partial homorganic stop. This is somewhat similar to the Anglophone's representing the fortis /l͈/ at the end of the Scottish Gaelic personal name *Domhnall* with a homorganic stop, thus producing the Anglicized form *Donald.*

The earliest examples of pre-occlusion of *n* in the Cornish texts are the three instances of *bedneth* 'blessing' in *Beunans Meriasek* (see below). Here are some fairly random examples from other documents:

> *me a vyden gewel* 'I will do' Loth 1900: 228; *pedn* 'head' RCEV: 97; *pidnian* 'brains' RCEV: 97; *brodn* 'teat' RCEV: 98; *pedn in nef* 'head in heaven' CW 182; *theth pedn ȝa gy* 'your head' CW 916; *mee a ved'n moze* 'I will go' BF: 15; *gwadnhez* 'weakened' BF: 25; *deu codna teer* 'two necks of land' BF: 25; *hedna* 'that' BF: 31; *warbedn denvith* 'against any man' BF: 42; *spladn* 'bright' BF: 43; *tedna akar* 'to pull away' BF: 43; *dadn daor* 'under ground' BF: 48; *dadn an ebron* 'under the sky' BF: 52; *an sterradnou* 'the stars' BF: 52; *tarednow* 'thunder-claps' ACB: F f *verso*; *bargidnia* 'to bargain' ACB: F f *verso*; *badna* 'a drop' ACB: F f 4; *gwadn* 'weak' ACB: F f 4.

In the later texts the pre-occluded element in disyllables became more pronounced and eventually swamped the following sonant. As a result one finds such forms as *hedda* LAM: 226, ACB: F f 3, BF: 43, for *hedna*.

11.2 The opposition *bedneth* ~ *banneth*

It should be noted, however, that not all dialects of Cornish appear to have pre-occluded *n* and *m*. Presumably in some forms of Cornish the difference betwen /n͈/ and /n/ was lost, both being reduced to /n/ before the Prosodic Shift. In such dialects pre-occlusion did not occur. In those dialects however the functional load, where possible, was transferred to the vowel. In dialects that did not pre-occlude, *benneth* 'blessing' and *benen* 'woman' would originally have had the same stressed vowel. When the opposition between /n͈/ and /n/ was lost, however, the vowel originally before /n͈/ was lowered from *e* to *a*. In non-occluding dialects, therefore, 'blessing' was *banneth*, whereas occluding dialects maintained the original vowel. When pre-occlusion began to be shown in writing, 'blessing' apppears as *bedneth*, *bednath*, but forms with stressed [a] are never pre-occluded. This can be seen from the distribution of the variants in the texts:

bedneth BM 198, 224, 225; *bedna* CW 1540; *bednath* RComm; *Bednath* ACB: E e 4 *verso*; *bedneth* ACB: E e 4 *verso*.

banneth BM 201, 506, 507, 534, 578, 581, 1011, 2509, CW 1871, AB: 240c; *bannath* BK 2897, 3048, 3055, 3114, CW 105.

Exactly the same complementary distribution is to be seen in Lhuyd's entries under *Is* 'He, the same' at AB: 73b, i.e. *hana* and *hedda*. The first represents the pronoun from a form of Cornish where pre-occlusion did not occur and in consequence the vowel was lowered; the second represents a dialect in which the vowel remained, pre-occlusion occurred and swamped the sonant. We thus have two distinct developments: *henna* > **hena* > *hana* and *henna* > *hedna* > *hedda*.

11.2.1 *mannaf* ~ *mydnaf*

In the *Creation of the World* a similar opposition is apparent between two different forms of the first person singular of *mynnes* 'to wish', A) those forms which have *i* or *y* in the stressed syllable and exibit pre-occlusion and B) those which contain *a* in the stressed syllable and are without pre-occlusion:

A

vidnaf CW 36; *vidna* CW 1154; *vydnaf* CW 1457.

B

vannaf CW 134, 507, 578, 648, 682, 1088, 1125, 1380, 1697, 2360; *manaf* CW 313, 471, 503; *mannaf* CW 314, 1362, 2231; *mannaff* CW 2180.

Since the forms with a stressed *a* are never pre-occluded, they are probably indicative of the dialect of Jordan's exemplar. This dialect would have been similar to that which said *banneth* 'blessing' and *hana* 'that man'. The forms in CW with *i* or *y* which show pre-occlusion probably represent his own dialect. Given the preponderance of pre-occlusion in place-names of the more westerly parts of Cornwall, we may surmise that the non-pre-occluding dialects were the more easterly ones.

11.3 Pre-occlusion of *m*

The pre-occlusion of *m* is different from that of *n* since there was no lenis *m* as a product of lenition. The lenition product of *m* was *v* (probably originally with a nasal element). It seems fair to assume that before the Prosodic Shift Cornish had a fortis *m,* which occurred at the beginning of a word, when the initial was not lenited and internally and finally as the reflex of earlier *-mm-*, for example in *mam* 'mother' < **mamma-*, or of *-mb-* in *kemer* 'take' < **kom + ber.* After the Shift initial *m* and *m* < *-mb-* or *-mm-* after an unstressed vowel, e.g. in *kemeres* 'to take' appeared as [m]. After stressed vowels *m* was pre-occluded to *bm*. As was the case with pre-occluded *n,* the stopped nature of pre-occluded *m* was weak to begin with and in consequence not shown in writing. In those forms of Cornish which did not pre-occlude *n, m* was not pre-occluded either.

Here are some examples of pre-occluded *m* from traditional Cornish:

> *na gybmar dowte* 'don't be afraid' CW 692;
> *tha vabm* 'your mother' CW 1203;
> *cabm* 'bent' CW 1603;
> *kebmys* 'so great' CW 1220;
> *obma* 'here' CW 2523;
> *kebmer uîth* 'take care' BF: 17;
> *Cabm-thavaz* 'rainbow' ACB: F f;
> *tubm* 'warm' ACB: F f 4;
> *tabm* 'a bit, a bite' ACB: F f 4.

We saw that in *hedna* the pre-occluded stop eventually swamped the original sonant to give *hedda*. The same thing appears to have happened with pre-occlude *m*. We thus find both *obma* 'here' e.g. CW 2523 and *obba* BF: 15 x 3, 16 x 2. Similarly *lebmyn* 'now' CW 70, 80 becomes *lebben* BF: 16, 25, 27.

11.4 *Alebma* 'hence'

The phrase *yn chymma* 'in this house' is attested at PC 667 and 1207. When the enclitic particle *-ma* is added to *chy,* a long and thus dimoric final syllable, the whole behaves as a single accentual group and the *chy* is shortened: [ən 'tʃi:mə] > [ən 'tʃɪmə] and to show that the stressed vowel is short, the following *m* is doubled. The same phrase occurs as *yn chemma* RD 1397. Here the vowel is demonstrably short, because short *i* and short *e* are in free variation in stressed open syllables. The same shortening happened with *le* 'place' in the phrase *a'n le-ma* 'from this place, hence', which regularly gives *alemma* OM 83, 169, PC 107, 153, RD 135, 151, etc. Later the *m* after a stressed short vowel is pre-occluded: *a lebma* CW 2080; *alebma* BF: 19. This development is, incidentally, excellent evidence that half-length had been eliminated from Middle Cornish and that long vowels were themselves dimoric. If the vowels in *chy* and *le* had been trimoric, before *-ma* they would both have lost a single mora to become half-long. In which case the phrase 'in this house' would have been written **yn chyma*. In the phrase and *a'n lema* the vowel would have been dimoric rather than short. It would not have been written *alemma*, nor could it have undergone pre-occlusion—since short vowels only are pre-occluded.

11.5 Further conditions in which pre-occlusion can occur

Historically speaking the word *un* 'one' did not contain *-nn-*, deriving as it does from IE **oyno-*. It appears, however, that when it occurs before a noun in a single phrasal unit, the final segment *-n* was strengthened to *-nn-* and thus could pre-occlude in Middle Cornish and Late Cornish. Here are some examples:

> *in vdn dew* 'in one God' CW 11;
> *vdn eall* 'an angel' CW 1753;
> *vdn spyes* 'a single moment' CW 1969;
> *in vdn rew* 'in a row' CW 2145;
> *vdn venyn* 'a woman' CW 2213;
> *na ve idn frôth* 'there was not a single rebuke' BF: 19;
> *do idn tellar* 'to one place' BF: 59.

It also appears that the yod [j], written ‹y› in nominal and verbal suffixes could also strenthen *n* to *nn* and thus provoke pre-occlusion:

> *pidnian* 'brains' RCEV: 97;
> *pymp cans a vlethydnyow* 'five hundred years' CW 1862;
> *dzhei a vargidniaz* 'they bargained' BF: 17;
> *fortidniez* 'fortunate' BF: 31;
> *bargidnia* 'to bargain' ACB: F f 1 *verso*.

11.6 Pre-occlusion as a progression

The swamping of the original sonant by the pre-occluded stop, i.e. *hedda* for *hedna* for *henna* 'that one', and *obba* for *obma* for *omma* 'here' are of particular interest. Swamping of this sort occurs only in disyllables where the pre-occluded consonant is followed immediately by schwa. It is also noteworthy that forms like *hedda* and *obba* seem to occur later than their precursors *hedna* and *obma*. This in itself suggests that the phenomenon of pre-occlusion involved a progression, from barely perceptible to overwhelming. It is the fact of this progression which explains why pre-occlusion, though probably present in some dialects much earlier, did not appear in writing until the sixteenth century.

The opposition between *bedneth* and *banneth* noted above may also help to explain the absence of pre-occlusion until relatively late. The failure of some dialects to pre-occlude implies that in them the difference between fortis /n͈/ and lenis /n/ was lost before pre-occlusion could occur. Presumably also in these dialects there would have been no phonetic difference in *m*, whatever its position, and thus pre-occlusion of *m* could not occur either. If as seems likely from toponymic evidence the pre-occluding dialects tended to be the western ones, it is likely that the dialects which did not pre-occlude were those of further to the east and were probably the more literary ones. If so, to begin with at least, pre-occlusion may have been considered rather sub-standard and scribes, whatever their own dialect, may have been reluctant to show pre-occlusion in writing.

11.7 Inconsistencies in writing pre-occlusion

One of the most remarkable features of pre-occlusion is the way in which the same scribe will write a word with pre-occlusion at one moment, and without it in the next sentence. Thus in Lhuyd's text of JCH he writes *varginiaz* 'bargained' in § 4 and § 7 but *vargidniaz* in § 9.

11.8 Variations in spelling

Some words are attested with pre-occlusion, e.g. *gwadn* 'weak', *brodn* 'breast', *gwydn* 'white'. Others are never attested with pre-occlusion, e.g. *man* 'anything', *gon* 'I know', *jyn* 'engine, device'. An adequate orthography for revived Cornish should certainly indicate which words may, and which may not, be pre-occluded.

CHAPTER 12

The graphs *gh, h,* and *wh* in Cornish

12.1 Initial [x] in the Brythonic languages

Cornish, like Welsh and Breton, will tolerate [x] at the end of syllable, e.g. W *sych* 'dry', B *sec'h* 'dry' and Cornish *segh, sygh* 'dry' OM 757, 761, 1100, PC 837, BK 1433. Welsh and Breton will also tolerate [x] at the beginning of a syllable, e.g., W *ei chalon* 'her heart', B *he c'halon* 'her heart'. Cornish on the other hand does not allow [x] initially but prefers [h], e.g. *hy holon* 'her heart' PA 224b, OM 2174, 2748. In this respect Cornish is similar to Middle English, which allows [x], written ‹gh› at the end of a syllable, e.g. *plough, plogh* 'plough', but does not allow [x] in initial position.

Cornish exhibits the same similarity to English with respect to original [xw]. Both Welsh and Breton exhibits [xw] in initial position, e.g. W *chwant* 'desire', B *c'hoant* 'desire', but Cornish *whans* 'desire' PA 1b, 222a, OM 91, etc.; W *chwys* 'perspiration', B *c'hwez* 'perspiration' but Cornish *whys* 'perspiration' OM 273, PC 2511, RD 245; W *chwi* 'you (pl.)', B *c'hwi* 'you' but Cornish *why* PC 1852, 1877, 2644, etc.

The simplest and most obvious explanation for the preference shown by Cornish for initial [h] and [ʍ] is that as a result of the Prosodic Shift the phonology of the language became assimilated in this respect to that of English.

12.2 Internal *-ch-* in Old Cornish

The word for 'poor' appears in Old Cornish as *bochodoc* OCV 297. The word derives from **bochod,* the antecedent of Middle Cornish *bohes* 'little, small amount'. In Middle Cornish 'poor' is *bohosek,* where the original [x] at the beginning of the second syllable has been reduced to [h]. This is the same phenomenon as has been noted in initial position. Middle Cornish will tolerate [x], written ‹gh› at the end of a word but at the beginning of a word, or internally at the beginning of a syllable [x] becomes [h].

One of the most obvious examples of this phonotactic preference in Middle Cornish is the word for 'small'. This appears as *boghan* in OCV 952. Nance spelt the word **byghan,* a form which is nowhere attested in any of the Middle Cornish texts. PA does, however, write *beghan* twice PA 53c and 166b, an idiosyncratic spelling since the word consists of two syllables, the second beginning with the medial consonant. We would therefore perhaps expect 'small' in Cornish to be spelt *byhan,* where [x] at the beginning of the internal syllable has been reduced to [h]. Indeed *byhan* is so spelt in the Ordinalia, e.g. OM 397, 810, 1269 and PC 91. The internal [h] seems to have been lost early, however, and the commonest way of spelling 'small' in the texts is *byan,* e.g. OM 1653, 1695, 2682, PC 2082, 2250, 2348, 3004, RD 1635, BM 257, 267; *byen,* e.g.

OM 806, RD 1029, BM 384, 1346, 1450, 1692, BM 2092, 2898; or *bean,* e.g. TH 4, 5, 19, 28a, 32, CW 118, 2481.

12.3 *-gh* at the end of a syllable

When a verbal stem ends in *-lgh,* this *-lgh* will stand at the end of the monosyllabic form of the verb. When, however, *lgh* is not final but is followed by a vowel, the *l* and the *gh* are in different syllables, and *gh* being at the beginning of its syllable is reduced to *h*. This phenonomenon can be clearly seen in the following examples involving parts of the verb *golhy* 'to wash':

golgh* but *golhy, golhys
me a wolgh 'I shall wash' PC 2499; *eff ath wolgh* 'he will wash you' BM 1795
golhy 'to wash' PC 518, 845, 862, 875, BM 745, 1600, 1716; *golhys* 'washed' PA 46d, PC 840, 857, 860, 861, RD 1929, BM 1493, 1496, 1520, 1822, 1832, 1481; *gulhis* 'washed' SA 60a; *ty ny's golhyth* 'you will not wash them' PC 853.

The same phenomenon can be observed in the verb for 'to hunt', but in this case the verbal noun is *helghya* which must be syllabified *helgh+ya* and thus has *-lgh* at the end of a syllable. The verbal adjective *helhys* on the other hand is to be syllabified *hel+hys* and in consequence the spelling exhibits *h* rather than *gh*:

helgh* and *helghya* but *helhys
My a'n helgh 'I will hunt him' BK 545; *me a'n helgh* BK 2696; *helghya* 'to hunt' BM: 3160, 3465, 3898.
helheys 'hunted' PA 2b; *helhys* 'hunted' OM 709, BM 2249.

When *-lgh* occurs at the end of a word, other than as part of a verb, *gh* is usually lost entirely. This can be seen in the word *kal* 'penis' BF: 58; AB 116c, 171c; cf. B *kalc'h,* and *Calesvol* 'Excalibur' BK 3269; cf. W *Caledfwlch.*

Although in certain cases analogy has restored *-gh-* at the beginning of syllable, it is a general that the Cornish scribes prefer *-h-* at the beginning of a syllable and *-gh* at the end. Here are some examples of this alternation:

flogh 'child' OM 300, 390, 397, 647, etc., PC 2929, RD 1364, BM 181, 192, 338, 846, 1550, etc., TH 9a, 23, 23a x 2, 25, 32a, etc., SA 59, CW 1837.
flehes 'children' OM 932, 1036, 1258, PC 2643, 2647, BM 2014, TH 7a, 22, 22a, 28, 28a, 42, 54a, Bilbao; *flehas* OM 975, 1031, 1159, 1168, BM 1780, 1699, 1782, 3153, TH 10a, ÉCII: 181, BF: 41; *flehys* PA 149d, 168c, OM 1623, BM 41, 94, 116, 183, 1119, 1321, 1507, etc., TH 9, BK 152, CW 653, 1035, 1061, 1614, 1979, 2210, 2227, etc.; *flehis* TH 23a x 2; 24, 26, 37, 37a, 41, 59, CW 1385.

trogh 'broken, cut' OM 298, PC 2687, 2185, RD 1244, 1365, BM 1279, 1570, 2840, 3046, 3353, 3585, 3831.

trehy 'to cut' OM 1010, 2445, 2502, 2519, PC 2561, BM 1620; *trehys* OM 2562, PC 2568.

yagh 'healthy, sound' PC 2681, 2694, RD 1671, BM 711, 713, 4121, 2439, TH 8a, BK 3040.

yehes 'health' PC 1150, BM 701, 2013, 2537; *yehas* TH 2a, 46, BK 2677, 3111; *ȝehas* BM 1681, 1686, 1694, 1703, 2645; *ehas* TH 51a.

The same alternation is seen in: *ef a vyth kyrhys* 'he will be fetched' OM 886 but *my a kyrgh an guas wharre* 'I will fetch the fellow straightway' at OM 887. It is also noteworthy that *arhans* 'silver' appears as *arans* as early as OM 2100. Note also the second plural imperative *kerugh* 'fetch!' for **kerheugh* at PC 1359. These last two spellings seem to indicate that the medial segment *-rh-* is simply a voiceless *r*.

It cannot be stressed enough that *-gh* in *flogh*, for example, and *-h-* in *flehes* do not represent the same phoneme. In *flogh* the graph *-gh* represents [x], whereas the *h* in *flehes* represents [h]. Since they are different phonemes, they should be spelt differently.

12.4 *forth* 'way' > *for*, *porth* 'port' > *por*

The word forth 'way, road' has a voiced final [ð] which is lost early: *in mes a pup for* 'out of every way' PC 2418; *an for na* 'that way' RD 2324; *an for ma* 'this way' BM 3251; *neb for* 'some way' CW 433, 454, 1233; *pynag[e]ll for* 'whichever way' CW 811; *ny won for thy* 'I do not know the way there' CW 1738.

Final [ð] is also frequently lost in *yn kerth* 'away, out': *ow kemeras e ker* 'taking away' SA 65a; *ke in ker* 'go hence' CW 712, 1208; *in ker vaggya* 'to journey away' CW 1335; *the doen in ker* 'to carry away' CW 2427; *nyedge in ker* 'fly away' CW 2451; *po 'rygo hwei moz ker* 'when you went away' BF: 19; *merwal akar* 'to die out' BF: 25, 29; *angye eath carr* 'they went away' ÉCII: 197; *gellez carr* 'gone away' ÉCII: 198. Similarly the final segment [ð] is lost in **hordh* 'ram' > *hor*'; cf. *Hor, hordh* glossing *Aries* 'ram' AB: 295b.

The final segment is also lost in *porth* 'port', but because it is voiceless [θ], it seems fair to assume that when it is lost, it devoices the preceding *r*: [porθ] > [por̥], e.g. *tuah Poreeah* 'towards St Ives' BF: 25; *Por Enez* 'Mousehole' AB: 222.

Internally *rth* [rθ] is often reduced to *rr* in *gorthyp* 'answer' and derivatives, e.g. *gorryb* 'answer' CW 1198, 1736, 1761; *tha orybe ge* 'your answer' SA 62; *an gorrybys* 'answered him' TH 20a; *gorrybowe* 'answer!' (pl.) CW 142.

The word *gwertha* 'to sell' appears as *Guerha* in the 'Pilchard Song' (BF: 44), where *-rha-* looks like an attempt to show the devoicing of *r* in writing. In the second version *gwertha* appears as *wharra* BF: 41, where the devoicing by metathesis appears in the first segment.

On occasion *-rth* is written by hypercorrection for *r* both internally and finally, e.g. *ow arluth merth* (for *ow arluth mer* 'my great lord') BK 2755; *gorthys* (for *gorrys* 'put') CW 2125; *gorthell* (for *gorhell* 'ship') CW 2255.

12.5 Confusion between *gh* and *th* medially and finally

We have noted above that Cornish tolerates [x] in at the end of a syllable. We thus find for example *flogh* 'child' OM 300, 390; *sagh* 'sack' BK 1024; *segh* 'dry' OM 757, 1100. Final [x] has a tendency to be lost, however, *flô* 'child' ÉCII: 196 x 2, 197, *sawe* 'load' TH 27a, ACB: F f 3 (‹ **sawgh*); *whe* 'six' PC 351, Bilbao (‹ **whegh*). We have also seen that final *rth* [rθ] is reduced to give [r̥]. As a result speakers were not always sure whether the final cluster in certain monosyllables, which was pronounced [r̥] should be written ‹rgh› or ‹rth›. We thus find considerable confusion: *de merth* 'thy daughter' (for *de mergh*) BF: 41, *y virth* 'his daughter' (for *y virgh*) TH 21a ; *kerth* 'oats' (for *kergh*) CW 1066; *marth* 'horse' (for *margh*) CW 406; *sownde a verth* 'sound of horses' (for *a vergh*) TH 56; *yrth* 'snow' (cf. *yrgh* BM 3055) TH 56a; and *warlerth* 'after' (for *warlergh*) TH 1 x 2,10, 18 x 2, 21, SA 65a, BK 3013, CW 1864.

The usual title of the Blessed Virgin Mary is *an Wyrhes Ker Marya,* e.g. at RD 154, 1200, TH 12a x 2. The first element of the name, however, is not infrequently written *Werthias* SA 64a, *Worthias* SA 61, 61a or *Worthyas* BK 158, where the cluster *-rth-* is for etymological *-rh-*.

In certain cases *-rth* is written by hypercorrection, when simple *r* would have been expected, e.g. *lowarth mamb* 'many mothers' SA 59; *lowarth onyn* 'many a one' SA 59a, 64; *lowarth gwyeth* 'many times' SA 61.

Rarely the confusion works the other way, i.e. with **rgh* for *rth*: *in nergh korf* (for *in nerth korf* 'in strength of body') BK 2369.

The confusion of *gh* and *th* extends to places where final [x] was immediately after a vowel. Thus, for example, we find *teer zeth* 'dry land' BF: 52 x 2.

12.6 *gh* before *t*

The Middle Cornish for 'king' is *myghtern,* which is stressed on the second syllable and where the group *ght* is [xt]. Spellings with ‹ght› gradually yield to spellings without ‹gh›. The spelling *myghtern,* however, is attested no fewer than 115 times. The persistence of ‹ght› in this word is remarkable, and it is likely that some of the scribes who wrote ‹myghtern› did so after the *gh* had ceased to be pronounced in their own speech. They were after all familiar with English spellings like *might, mighty, night, eight,* etc. in which the ‹gh› was quiescent. By the Late Cornish period the word was not merely spelt without ‹gh› but the neutral nature of the first and unstressed syllable was clear from the way it was spelt with *a*. Examples of *myghtern* are so numerous I list here only a selection of occurrences (I ignore capital letters and initial mutation in these lists):

mygtern PA 102c, 102d, 108b, 111d, 121d, 136c, 137c, 146d, 147c, 148b, 148d, 187d, 188b, 189d, 236d.

myghtern OM 1479, 1712, 2014, 2114, PC, 164, 276, 427, 1583, etc., RD 104, 105, 123, 173, BK 53, 1280, 1305, 1314, 1336, etc..

mytern BM 169, 223, 303, 548, 2463, 2464, 2465, 2588, 3177, 3196, TH 31, 51 x 2; *myterne* BM 4, TH 8a, BK 2420; *miterne* TH 13a, 31

matern ÉCII: 194 x 3, 194; *materne* LAM 224; *mattern* LAM: 224; *materen* LAM: 224, 226 x 2.

The scribe of PA writes *mygtern* throughout. This, one presumes, is his idiosyncratic spelling of *myghtern*. The most frequent use of the spelling *myghtern* is in *Bewnans Ke*. This may reflect the early date of the composition of the play (probably during the reign of Henry VI) and thus not far removed from the putative date of the Ordinalia, or it may be indicative of the rather elevated style of the second part of the play. Even so BK has one example of *vyterne*. Given that spellings with *-yt-* rather than *-yght-* are the rule from the period of *Beunans Meriasek* onward (i.e. AD 1504), we can be sure that the medial segment in *myghtern* had been simplified to *-t-* by the sixteenth century at the latest. Indeed the spelling *a ȝyttyas* 'prepared, arranged' at PA 3a (see below), suggests that when stressed, the cluster [xt] was weakening to [t]. This may indicate that forms of the word for 'king' with [t] rather than [xt] occurred in speech even earlier than BM, but were not shown in writing.

In the two common etyma *syght* 'sight' and *dyghtya* 'to treat' the cluster *-ght-* occurs after a stressed vowel. In the first *syght* [sɪxt] probably continued to be pronounced with internal [xt], i.e. in the form in which it had been borrowed into Cornish. The same would be true of the word *bryght* 'bright' which is attested twice: OM 771 and BM 1727. In BM the word rhymes with *syght* and is almost certain to have been pronounced [brɪxt].

The verb *dyghtye, dyghtya* 'to treat, to deal with' < ME *dighten* is fairly well attested in the Middle Cornish texts:

a ȝyttyas PA 3a; *dyȝgthtyas* PA 71d, *dyȝgthtys* PA 133a; *dyȝgtis* PA 141d, 153a, 163c, PA 219d; *dygtis* PA 165a, 177b; *dygtye* PA 199a; *dyȝgtys* PA 202a; *omȝyghtyn* PA 246d; *dyȝgtyas* PA 235d; *me a'n dygth* PC 624; *dyghtys* PC 692, 2605, 2634, 2926, 2945, 3189, BM 1280, BK 1130; *dyghtijs* BM 1415; *dytht* BK 1114.

It is likely that *dyghtys* 'treated' was pronounced ['dɪxtɪs]. The scribe of PA seems at the beginning of his text to be unsure how to spell the word. His written consonant cluster ‹ȝgtht› seems a little excessive to represent ‹xt› and is probably graphemic only. He represents the same cluster as ‹gt› in *mygtern* 'king'. He appears to simplify his spelling of *dyghtya* throughout PA. The spellings *ȝyttyas* 'prepared' at PA 3, however, and *dytht* 'get ready' at BK 1114 seem to suggest that in *-ght-* the velar fricative was already being lost. This is perhaps evidence that the velar fricative in *mygtern* 'king' was also being lost in PA.

12.7 Loss of internal *-th-* [ð]

Intervocalic *-th-* [ð] is lost in certain contexts. For example the adjective *efrethek* 'lame' in BM 540, 564, 684, 4520, appears as *effreg* in TH 44a x 2, 57a x 2. The original -th- [ð] is lost in the tetrasyllabic adjective 'loving', for the word still seems to retain four syllables after the loss of [ð]: *kerengeak* TH 2a, 10a, 11a, *kerengyek* TH 10a, *kerengyak* 30a x 2. In *kernsyak* TH 41 the second syllable has been elided, but the ending *-syak* < **-sethek* remains disyllabic.

In Late Cornish internal *-th-* [ð] is lost in the imperfect of *gothfos* 'to know', e.g. *an gie oyah teler an gye en noath* 'they knew that they were naked' ÉCII: 177; *eue a wya dro Gevern* 'he knew about Gevern' BF: 25.

12.8 *-gth-* in prepositional pronouns

The third person singular and plural of the prepositional pronouns *rag* and *thyrag* end in *-gth-* where the *th* is voiceless and tends to devoice the preceding *g* > *c*. This can be seen from the attested forms:

'for him, for it': *ractha* CW 379, 820, 1991, 2015, 2058; *ragta, ragthe* AB: 244b; *ragta* AB 352a , §§28 and 32.

'before him'*: deracta* BF: 39.

'before them': *deractanze* ÉCII: 196; *ragt'angi* LAM: 238.

There is no evidence for **ragdho* 'for him', **rygdhy* 'for her or **ragdha(ns)* 'for them' in Cornish of any period.

CHAPTER 13

Unexpected consonantal spellings

13.1 ‹th› for final ‹s›

Three words borrowed from ME, *fas* 'face', *gras* 'grace', *plas* 'place' and *spas* 'space, opportunity' which end in a voiceless [s] are frequently spelt with final ‹th› in the texts. I have collected the following instances:

***fas* 'face'**
fath OM 896, 1412, PC 1401, RD 1736, BM 944, 3412; *feth* PA 200c, 216c.

***gras* 'grace'**
grath OM 6, 263, 495, 623, 669, 680, 976, 1085, 1413, 1463, 1472, 2019, 2253, PC 4, 291, 1404; RD 252, 821, BM 346, 2081, 3475; *grayth* PA 222d.

***plath* 'place'**
plath OM 2080, 2091, PC 291, 2303, 2189, BM 946.

***spath* 'space, opportunity'**
spath BM 942.

In the verb 'to rise again' the segment following the first syllable is *-ss-* from earlier *d* + *s* and is voiceless. It is usually written ‹ss›:

'to rise again'
dasserhy PC 3085, RD 683, 942; *dasserhys* RD 665, 692, 939; *dasserghy* RD 61, 957, 1028; *dasserghys* RD 728, 799, 808, 895, 1004, 1039, 1065, 1214; *y tasserhy* PC 1747; *a tassergh* PC 1754; *y tasserghy* RD 375, 1193; *y tasserghys* RD 1146; *tassorgho* RD 379; *y tassorghas* RD 516; *mar tassorhas* RD 687.

On occasion, however, the voiceless *s* is written ‹th›:

dathergy RD 5, 7; *datherghys* RD 475, 481; *datherhys* 567; *e tathorhas* BK 311

Cf. also *dathserghys* RD 1462. The use of ‹th› for voiceless [s] might suggest that the segment was cacuminal or could be pronounced as a cacuminal *s*, and that this was sufficiently close to *th* [θ], to be written as such. In which case *y wleth* 'his kingdom' for *y wlas* at OM 2370 seems anomalous.

The confusion between voiceless *th* [θ] works the other way in *prag na thesons y yn chy* 'why have they not come into the house?' PC 1247, where *na thesons* is for *na thethons*.

13.2 *Dotho* 'to him', *dethy* 'to her', etc.

In Late Cornish texts the pronominal forms of the Middle Cornish preposition *the* with initial *d* rather than *th* [ð]. Thus 'to me' is *dym*, 'to you' is *dys*, 'to him' is *dotha*, etc. These items with initial *d* for *th* [ð] are not innovations, but are in fact are reflexes of the historical forms.

The original form of the simple preposition was probably *do, da*; cf. *do, da* in Old Breton. On this were based the Cornish forms *dym* 'to me', *dys* 'to thee', *dyn* 'to us' and *deugh* 'to you (pl). The third person singular feminine and plural contain an element *-eth-*, which appears again in *warnethy* 'upon her', *warnetha* 'upon them'. The third singular masculine was probably **detho* originally (cf. Middle Breton *deza, d'ezhan* 'to him'), but was reshaped by vocalic harmony to *dotho*. The initial *d-* was also assimilated to the medial segment to give Middle Cornish *thotho* ['ðɔðɔ]. Thereafter the fricative initial was generalized both to the pronominal forms *thym, thys, thethy, theugh* and *thetha*, and also to the simplex *the* 'to'. Forms with initial ‹d› however did not disappear and indeed are common in some texts, notably in *Beunans Meriasek*.

Here are some Middle and Late Cornish instances the prepositional pronouns 'to me', 'to thee', etc. with initial ‹d›:

dym 'to me' BM 536, 952, 1162, 1383, 1439, 1458, etc.; *dem* BF: 16, LAM: 238 x 2.
dys 'to thee' BM 63, 409, 529, 558, 643, 692, 1703, etc.; *des* BM 375, BF: 41; *dis* BM 415, 506, 532, 735, 912, 939, 1175, 2805, etc.
dotho 'to him' OM 741, 1094, 2238, PC 29, 248, 793, 1827, 2081, 2218, 2519, RD 603, 1445, BM 485, 549, 715, 1454, 1506, 1694, 2130, etc.; *doȝo* PA 146c, 173d, 208d; *dotha* BM 466, 1950, 2854, 3614; CW 1017, BF: 15, 25, 43, 44, 48 x 2, 59.
dethy 'to her' PC 529, 2202, 2562, BM 3122, 3693, 3695, 3707, 3708, 3780, 3945, 4278, CW 904.
dyn 'to us' BM 689, 1344, 1753, 2355, 2717, 2795, 3112, 3129, 3275, 3294, 4092; *dynny* BM 2715; *dyny* BM 2138; *den* BF: 25
dyugh 'to you' BM 767, 807, 1076, 1301, 1507, 2891, 3126, 3196, 3474, 3816, 3930, 4368; *dywhy* BM 2264, 2775, 2896, 3141, 3148; *dywy* BM 1698.
detha 'to them' BM 2955, 3307, 3534, 4556; *dethe* BM 1988; *dethy* 'to them' BM 3122; *dothans* CW 967, BF: 41, 53.

These synthetic parts of the preposition pronoun give way to variants made from the preposition itself followed by a suffixed pronoun. Some of these analytic forms also exhibit initial ‹d› rather than ‹th›:

do ve 'to me' ACB: F f 3; *de vy* 'to me' Loth 1900; *de vi* 'to me' Loth 1900 x 2
do ny 'to us' BF: 41 x 2
do vy 'to you' BF: 53; *do why* BF: 12, LAM: 238.

13.3 The alternation *v* ~ *w*

The sound written ‹v› was probably a voiced bilabial fricative [β], whereas ‹w› was probably a voiced bilabial approximant [w]. If contact between the lips when articulating [β] is reduced, [w] results, and there is good evidence that this happened in Middle and Late Cornish.

13.4 *Cavos* ~ *cawas* 'to get'

The most obvious example of the hesitation between [v] and [w] can be seen in the verbal noun of the verb 'to get'. There is a common form with intervocalic *-f-*: *cafos, caffos, cafus, caffus*. This corresponds to MB *caffout*. Then there is a form *cavos*, corresponding to MB *kavout*. The two stems are widely attested in Cornish, but the second form *cavos* alternates with a form *cawas* (or with permanent lenition *gawas*) and forms with *-w-* are more numerous than those with *-v-*. I have collected the following instances:

'to get' with *-v-*
cavos CW 1515; *kavaz* BF: 27, AB: 248a, 250b; *e gavaz* RC 23: 196.

'to get' with *-w-*
cawys RD 157; *cawas* BM 85, 255, CW 959, 1034, 1133, 1221, RComm.; *tha gawas* CW 1081, 2141; *gawas* CW 205, ACB: F f *verso*; *e gowis* SA 60; *gowas* ACB: F f 3 x 2, RComm.

13.5 Further instances of alternation of *v* and *w*

Elsewhere expected ‹v› not infrequently appears as ‹w› and vice versa. Here are some examples from the texts:

Expected [v] written ‹w›
a wur speys (for *a ver speys* 'in a short time') BM 688; *amuwys* (for *amuvys* 'excited') BM 1311; *age barwov* (for *age barvov* 'their beards') BM 2309; *dewysyow* (for *devysyow* 'sheep') BM 2981; *deworijs* (for *devorijs* 'devoured') BM 4179; *dynwyn* (for *dynvyn* 'to send) TH 35a; *a rug ow dynwyn ve* (for *a rug ow dynvyn ve* 'who sent me') TH 41a; *ponwotter* (for *ponvotter* 'misery') BK 425; *orth an wrusyl* (for *orth an vresel* 'for the insubordination') BK 969; *unwerhys* (for *unverhys* 'of one accord') BK 1035; *i wer onowr* (for *y ver onowr* 'its great honour') BK 1948; *wesper* (for *vesper* 'vespers') BK 2021; *e wos assys war en tron* (for *e vos assys war en tron* 'his being seated on the throne') BK 2279; *a'n prenwyth* (for *a'n prenvyth* 'will pay for it') BK 2577, 3077; *why a wylwyth* (for *why a wylvyth*

'you will see') BK 2725; *Gwynewer, Guynuwer* (for *Gwynnever* 'Guinevere') BK 3000, 30006 and 2741, 3135; *hewwall tha thew* (for *huvel tha thew* 'humble to God') SA 65a; *a awas* (for *a avas* 'forgave') CW 2044; *dell ewa dewar theny* (for *dell ewa devar theny* 'as it is our duty') CW 2328.

Expected [w] or [wh] written ‹v›

the vothfes (for *the wothfes* 'to know') BM 3259; *vastya boys* (for *wastya boys* 'to waste food') BM 3613; *var off* (for *war off* 'I am aware') BM 4014; *ny von* (for *ny won* 'I do not know) BM 4186; *na vith neffra duvuthys* (for *na vith neffra duwuthys* 'which will never be finished') BK 2198; *e tho hynvis* (for *e tho hynwis* 'it was called') SA 61a; *an moiha looan varbarr* (for *an moiha looan warbarr* 'the happiest together') BF: 16; *vor duath* (for *wor duath* 'finally') BF: 16; *Den fir o vi* (for *Den fir o whi* 'you are a wise man') BF: 46; *var budgeth an dour* (for *war budgeth an dour* 'upon the face of the water') BF: 51; *var an ebron* (for *war an ebron* 'upon the heaven') BF: 52; *kentel var bar an dour* (for *kentel warbar an dour* 'the gathering together of the water') BF: 52; *aveth* (for *aweth* 'also') BF: 52; *varler a haval* (for *warler a haval* 'after its kind') BF: 51 x 3; *varler haval ni* (for *warler haval ni* 'according to our kind') BF: 52; *var ol budgeth an aor* (for *war oll budgeth an aor* 'on all the face of the earth') BF: 53; *var an aor* (for *war an aor* 'upon the earth') BF: 53; *ma res gennam do vy* (for *ma res gennam do why* 'I have given you') BF: 53; *vor an fleaz* (for *wor an fleaz* 'upon the children') BF: 55; *vor an beau ha maro* (for *wor an beau ha marow* 'upon the living and the dead') BF: 56

It will be noted that writing *v* for expected *w* is a common Late Cornish phenomenon.

13.6 Loss of initial *w*

It has been noted at 6.3.2 above that *w* immediately after *d* was not sufficient to prevent assibilation. It has also been observed that following assibilated *g* (from *d*) *w* was lost, e.g. in *pager* 'four' (for **pegwar*) and in **aja-* 'gap' < **adwy* in toponyms. The weakness of Cornish *w* at the beginning of a syllable is noticeable elsewhere. The most frequent instance is that of initial *wr-*, which was reduced to *r-* at an early period. This is common in the lenited forms of the verb *gul* 'to do'. The forms *a wra* 'will do' and *a wruk, a wrug* 'did,' for example, are found throughout Middle Cornish. The Creation of the World has *wrug* or *wruge* throughout. Nonetheless *ra* and *ruk, rug* are common from the earliest period:

'will do'

a ra PA 39b, 60d, 63d, OM 203, 248, 1016, 1075, 2310, BM 612, 804, 822, 978, 1107, 1228, etc.

'did'

a ruk OM 182, 2426, BM 949, 2537, 2746, 2792, 3360, 3604, 4219, 4317, 4516, SA 61, 64a, 65a x 2; *a rug* PA 7d, 28b, 30d, 117a, 118d, 162c, 229c, TH 1a, 2, 2a x 4, 3 x 3, 3a, 4 x 2, etc., SA 60, 61, 63a, BK 138, 219, 232, 612, 688, 726, 786 (stage direction), 1096, 3148, 3154, CW 496; *a ruke* SA 64 x 2.

Tregear writes neither *a wra* nor *a wrug* but only *a ra* and *a rug*. In Late Cornish *a wrug*/*a rug* appears as *a rig* or *rig*. There are apparently no examples in the later language of *a *wrig*, and it seems likely that by the seventeenth century the initial *w* in *a wra, a wrug* has been lost entirely.

When the initial *g* of items beginning in *go-* is lenited, in Middle Cornish as a rule the lenited form begins with *wo-*. Thus we find *gothfos* OM 822, RD 468, 1203 but *the wothfos* OM 751. In the later language this *w* before the high back vowel is not infrequently lost. Here are some examples:

***gooth* 'pride', *gothys* 'proud'**

ȝa oth (for *ȝa woth* 'your pride') CW 233; *re othys* (for *re wothys* 'too proud') CW 306.

***gothfos* 'to know'**

tha othvas (for *tha othvas* 'to know') CW 646; *da othaz* (for *da wothaz* 'to know') RC23: 184; *a vffya* (for *a wuffya* 'would know') CW 598; *a orama* (for *a worama* 'that I know') BF: 27, 29; *na ora vee* (for *na wora' vee* 'I don't know') BF: 29; *Me a aore* (for *Me a wore* 'I know) BF: 31; *Deew a ore* (for *Deew a wore* 'God knows) RC 23: 176; *N'ora vi skrefa* (For *Na wora vi skrefa* 'I cannot write') AB: 250b.

***goky* 'foolish'**

mar ucky (for *mar wucky* 'so foolish') CW 815

***gorthyp* 'answer'**

tha orybe gee 'your answer' SA 62.

***guthyl* 'to do'**

ȝe vȝyll (for *ȝe wvȝyll*) BM 132.

In the later language the preposition and conjuncton *woge, wosa* 'after' sometimes loses the initial *w-*.

bus osa an consecration 'but after the consecration' SA 61a; *bus osa the vos consecratis* 'but after being consecrated' SA 62; *a ve ouga nena gwage* 'he was after that hungry' RC 23: 186; *rag ugge an Teez goth tho merwal akar* 'for after the old men die out' BF: 25; *ugge hemma* 'hereafter' BF: 27, 31;

ha ugge hedda 'and thereafter' BF: 29; *ugge hedna* 'thereafter' BF: 29; *Vdg' hedda* 'Thereafter' BF: 43; *Udg' hedda* 'Thereafter' BF: 44.

13.7 Voicing of *wh* > *w*

Although voiceless *w* is usually written ‹wh› in the Middle Cornish texts, it seems that the voicelessness is either not shown in writing on occasion, or more probably lost in speech. Here are some examples of ‹w› where ‹wh› would be expected:

'to seek'
ȝe welas 'to seek' PA 94d; *the weles* 'to seek' BM 1075; *rag weles* 'in order to seek' BM 2758; *na wyle* 'do not seek' 860, 3506; *na wyla* 'do not seek' BM 918; *pandra wyla* 'what does he seek?' BM 2362; *maran wyla* 'if he seeks it' BM 2744.

'to perspire; perspiration'
ef a wese 'he was perspiring' PA 58c; *I wysce a'th face* 'in the sweat of thy brow' TH 6.

'sweet, dear'
wek PA 132c, 193c, 257d, OM 86, 166, BM 24, 53, 66, 87, 114, 286, 298, 329, 347, 424, etc.

'desirous'
wensys (for *whensys*) SA 64a.

'harsh, unpleasant'
anwek BK 1506, 1508.

It seems likely that ‹w› for ‹wh› represents the phonetic reality of a voiced approximant, since on occasion ‹wh› is written by hypercorrection where ‹w› would be expected:

whare whosa mabden the beha 'immediately after mankind sinned' TH 13a
an pith a whrella ganow cowse 'the thing which mouth would speak' SA 61a.

13.8 Loss of initial *y*

From the earliest period it seems that initial [je], written ‹ye› is reduced in some texts to [e]. Here are some instances:

'Jew, Jews'
yethow 'Jew' PC 2003, 2027; *yethewon* 'Jews' PC 1080, 1098, 1111, 1252, 1521, 1548, 1565, etc.; *yethewen* 'Jews' PC 2796, 2797, 2800; *ȝethewon*

'Jews' BM 2602, 2990; *yuthewon* PC 982 [this form has apparently arison by vocalic metathesis].

ethow 'Jew' PA 131a, 152a, 183a; *eȝow* 'Jew' PA 145c, 239b; *eȝewon* 'Jews' PA 33a, 38d, 63a, 69a, 81a, 90a, 103c, etc.; a*n nethewan* 'the Jews' SA 61 x 2; *an Ethewan* 'the Jews' RC 23: 194, 200; *Edheuon* 'Jews' AB: 73c; *Edhewon* 'Jews' AB: 230a; *Idheuon* 'Jews' AB: 242c.

'health'

yehes PC 1150, BM 701, 2013, 2537; *yeghes* RD 1716; *yehas* TH 2a, 46, BK 2677, 3111; *ȝehes* BM 3073, 4221, 4231.

ehas 'health' TH 51a; *eghas* TH 30a; *ehaz* AB: 242a, ACB F f *verso*, F f 4 x 2; *Ehaz* CPT: 11.

'language'

**yeth* 'language' is not attested, but initial *y* is expected; cf. W *iaith* 'language' and B *yezh* 'language'

eyth 'language' TH 1, 19, 21, 40, 57a.

'to desire; desire'

yenes 'desire' OM 2125, PC 1046; *me re yevnys* 'I have desired' PC 1701

ny vnsa 'he would not wish' PA 21d; *ewnadow* 'desire' BM 30; *unadow* 'desire' BK 574, 628, 730, 1619, 2036, 2947; *vny* 'to desire' TH 22a, 30.

'cold'

yeyn PC 1209, 1215, 1622, 2729; *yen* PC 2060; *yeyne* CW 1262; *yeine* ACB F f 3.

eyn PA 207d, 235d; *yne* BM 1145.

From Caradar's day onwards some commentators have believed that the name spelt ‹ihesu› or ‹iesus› in the Middle Cornish texts should be understood as **Yesu*, by analogy with Welsh *Iesu*. There are several reasons for rejecting this suggestion (see GG: 221-23). If the name of Our Saviour had really been **Yesu* in Middle Cornish, we would expect to find instances in which the initial ‹y› [j] had been lost. Since *ihesu* and *ihesus* are attested more than 500 times and yet there are no instances of **esus* or **esu*, it seems reasonable to conclude that the initial segment was not [j]. Without doubt the name *Ihesu*(*s*) 'Jesus, Jesu' in Middle Cornish had initial [dʒ].

CHAPTER 14
Orthographic considerations

14.1 Short unstressed high front vowels before *-n*

Although the present work is largely concerned with the consonants of traditional Cornish, I should like at this point to draw attention to the various spellings of a number of relatively common etyma ending in *-yn* or *-en* in the Middle Cornish texts.

A

1) **'now'**

lemmyn PA 12c, 51a, 60a, 61b, 69d, 75c, 78c, 92c, 125c, 182c, etc., OM 656, 1306, 1310, 1323,1341, 1349, 1396, 1654, PC 1242, 1255, 1275, 1369, 1377, 1382, 1413, etc., RD 27, 86, 149, 170, 179, 289, 361, 445, 501, etc., BM 11, 138, 173, 212, 4000, TH 1a, SA 60, BK 477, 769, 783, 797, 880, 1223, 1818, 1870, 2787, 2985; *lebmyn* CW 70, 80, 2091, 2240, 2487; *lymmyn* PA 87c, 139d, OM 2839, PC 1079, 1149, 1194, 2146, TH 1a, 2, 3a, 4, 5, 11a, 13, 16, 16a, 18, etc., SA 61, BK 759.

lemmen PC 1913, BM 57, 703, 941, 1135, 1363, 1830, 2493, 2794, etc., SA 62, BK 191, 521, 603; *lemen* BM 720, 1819, 1834, 1967, 2185, 2209, 2354, etc. Notice also *lemman* PA 245d, PC 82, PC 307, PC 762, 918, 1304, 2144, 2451, BM 2297, 3542.

2) **'time'**

termyn PA 48c, 66d, 75c, OM 351, 686, 1360, 1362, 1441, 1748, 2076, 2345, PC 703, 790, 819, 1040, 1053, 1539, 1654, 1690, etc., RD 352, 706, 747, 1053, 1112, 1312, 1349, 1852, BM 141, 532, 1741, TH 2a, 19a, 49a, BK 321, 826, 865, 2037, 3240, CW 88, 592, 1671, 1893, 1914, 2116, 2209; *tyrmyn* OM 45, TH 11a, 13a, 14 x 2, 15, 16a, 17, 18a, 21a, 24, etc., BK 1209; *tirmyn* TH 48, 52, SA 60.

termen BM 447, 513, 592, 1223, 1920, 2024, 2032, 2179, 2736, 2837; *a dermen* BM 2502.

3) **'sign, token'**

tokyn OM 1243, 1247, PC 343, 971, 984, 1081, 1781, 2497, BM 3425, TH 28a, 57, BK 2026, 2048.

token OM 1733, 2659, CW 1181, 1644.

B

1) **'splendid, noble'**
brentyn BM 1528, 1650, CW 2242; *bryntyn* OM 1962, 2281, 2420, PC 1542, BK 1180.

There are no instances with final *-en*.

2) **'kitchen'**
i'n gegyn 'in the kitchen' BM 3721.
i'n gegen 'in the kitchen' BM 3928; *than gegen* 'to the kitchen' CW 2012.

3) **'Latin'**
latyn TH 57a.
laten BM 81.

4) **'mill'**
Kewnans an Velyn BK 1197, 1202 (stage direction).

There are no instances with final *-en*.

5) **'morning'**
myttyn PA 243a, OM 2074, 2279, 2307, 2424, PC 2680, BK 827, 2744; *du fencost myttyn* 'on the morning of Pentecost' TH 44a
mo ha meten 'evening and morning' BM 2738; *du gwener vetten* 'Friday morning' BM 4420.

All eight etyma (A 1-3 and B 1-5) are spelt in Middle Cornish with *-yn* or *-en*. In the revived language all are pronounced with exactly the same unstressed syllable [ɪn] or [ən]. In any well-designed orthography for revived Cornish all eight would be spelt with final ‹yn› (with ‹en› possibly as a late variant): *lemmyn* or *lebmyn, termyn, tokyn, bryntyn* or *brentyn, kegyn, Latyn, melyn* and *myttyn*. Not only are etymological spellings in *-in* for some of the above inauthentic, but they introduce unnecessary complication into the orthography of the revived language.

14.2 The alternation *y* ~ *e* in the Cornish for 'book'

At 9.1 above I cited some of the various spellings of the Cornish word for 'book.' I should like here to list all the attested spellings of the singular of the word in the Middle Cornish texts, separating them into two classes, 1) those with ‹y› in the first syllable and 2) those that have ‹e›:

1) ***lyver*, etc.**
lyuer TH 18a, 55; *lyver* TH 6a, 42, 45a, 47a, 49a, SA 60; *lyvyr* PC 95; *lyfer* TH 45; *lyffer* TH 18a.

2) ***lever*****, etc.**

leuer TH 50a; *lever* TH 1a, 46a x 2, 47a x 2, SA 61a, 62a, 63a; *levar* PA 135d, TH 56a, SA 59; *levyr* PC 1157, TH 48a, 49, 55a, 56; *lefer* BM 1418, 1499.

It seems that there are 11 forms with ‹y› in the first syllable to be found in the Middle Cornish texts and no fewer than 17 instances with ‹e› as the stressed vowel. It is difficult therefore to maintain that *lyver* is a Middle Cornish spelling and *lever* Late Cornish, for *lever* is already commoner than *lyver* in the Middle Cornish texts.

The same variation can be seen between *tyller* 'place' and its variant *teller.* Here are some of the attested forms:

1) ***tyller*** **etc.**

tyller PA 18a, 33a, 65a, 176a, 250b, OM 1551, 1992, 2045, PC 86, 106, 980, 1103, 1837, 2597, RD 270, TH 16, 42a, 43a, 45, 47 x 3, BK 149; *tyllar* TH 6, 18, 29a, 42, 42a, 53; *tillar* SA 65a, 66

2) ***teller*****, etc.**

teller PA 206d, OM 579, 939, 1095, 1823, 1909, 2275, 2795, PC 501, BM 629, 677, 1145, 2922, TH 2, 44; *tellar* TH 32, 32a, 35a, 45, BK 2977, CW 866, 871, 1157, 1848.

Forms with ‹e› in the stressed vowel are almost as common in the Middle Cornish texts as forms with ‹y› or ‹i›. One cannot therefore claim that *teller, tellar* are distinctively Late forms. There is therefore no justification for insisting upon such a distinction in the revived language.

CHAPTER 15
Initial *J*- in biblical names

15.1 The biblical name for 'John'

Caradar appears to have believed that 'John' in the New Testament should have been spelt ‹Yowan› in revived Cornish. This was almost certainly a mistake. He also spelt the name for 'Jesus, Jesu' as ‹Yesu›. This too was a mistake and as we have seen at 13.8 above the absence of forms without initial ‹Y› are strong evidence against Caradar's opinion. There are further reasons to be sceptical of ‹Yesu›, however (see 15.2 below).

Comparison with Breton *Yann* 'John' and Welsh *Ieuan* 'John' led Caradar to believe that ‹Iowan› in the Cornish texts had initial [j] and in consequence he spelt the name *Yowan*. Some have followed him in this matter. There are several reasons for not doing so, however:

a) The commonest spelling for 'John' in Cornish is ‹iowan› or ‹Iowan›, e.g. PA 53a, 198c, PC 700, 2928, RD 949. In *Passio Christi* we read: *ol sav peder ha jamys ha johann an try a reys mones gynef yredy* 'all except Peter and James and John, the three must go with me indeed' PC 1014-16. *Johann* here is a variant spelling for ‹iowan›. A similar spelling is found in *iohan nynsos lemmyn flogh* 'John, you are not now a child' RD 1364. In the first quotation above *johann* begins with ‹j› and is mentioned immediately after *jamys*, which also begins with a ‹j›. *Jamys* is quite obviously a borrowing from Middle English, where the name has an initial [dʒ]. In English the two names *James* and *John* alliterate, as they do in Latin also, e.g. *vidit alios duos fratres, Jacobum Zebedaei, et Joannem fratrem ejus* 'he saw to further brothers, James son of Zebedee and John his brother' Matt. 4.21. It is likely therefore that in Cornish *jamys* and *iowan, johann, johan* alliterated also. In which case Cornish *Iowan* is to be understood as having an initial [dʒ].[1]
b) William Rowe translates Matt. 4.21: *Ha moaze a lenna e a wellaz moy deavw broderath, James mab Zebde ha Jowan e broder en goral gen Zebde go zeerah* 'And going thence he saw two more brothers, James the son of Zebedee and John his brother in the boat with Zebedee their father' ÉCII: 191-92. *James mab Zebde ha Jowan e broder* are obviously the same names as seen at PC 1014-16; moreover since they are spelt

1 Editor's note: In most medieval Cornish hands upper-case *I* and *J* are not distinguishable, and indeed are not distinguished; neither are lower-case *i* and *j*, except where the latter appears as a swash in *iij* 'three' or in terminations like *-ijs* (= *-ys*).

with the same initial, they clearly alliterate. This is further evidence that 'John' in the New Testament has initial *J* not *Y* in Cornish.

c) In secular texts 'John' in Cornish has initial ‹J› pronounced [dʒ]. We know this from Lhuyd's semi-phonetic rendering of the folktale 'Jowan Chy an Hordh'. Lhuyd throughout writes the name *Jowan* as ‹Dzhûan›, where the initial is clearly [dʒ]. This corresponds exactly with John Boson's form *Jooan* 'John'.
d) The scribe of BM spells the Cornish for 'St John the Baptist' as *sen iowen baptyst* BM 4450. This is patently the same name as that written by Tregear as *S. Johan baptist* TH 8, *S Johan baptist* TH 29a and *Jowan baptist* TH 43a. It seems clear that the saint's name begins with *J*, pronounced [dʒ].
e) If the name for 'John' really began with [j], we would expect to find instances of it in the texts beginning with ‹Y›, after all Cornish some words begin with ‹yo›, e.g. *yowynk* 'young' PC 19, 39, BM 1196; *yonk* 'young' PA 175c, PC 1184, BM 3659 and *yov* 'Thursday' BM 1472. No spelling ‹yowan› or the like is attested anywhere.

It is likely that during the Saxon domination of Cornwall in the tenth and eleventh centuries, many of the original names for characters in the Bible were lost. Their absence was made good after the Norman Conquest by borrowings from French, Breton and English. The original name for any John in the New Testament would have been **Iowan* or similar < Latin *Iohannes;* this was the origin of Breton *Yann*. Such a form seems to survive only in the expression *Golowan* 'Midsummer' < *gool Owan* 'festival of St John,' seen in the *Gwâve en Hâve terebah Goluan, ha Hâve en Guâve terebah Nadelack* 'Winter in summer till Midsummer, and summer in winter until Christmas' (CPT: 11).

Although Caradar believed that 'John' should be rendered *Yowan* in the New Testament and indeed elsewhere, not everybody followed him. In his version of the Gospel of St Matthew (*An Awayl herwyth Sen Mathew*) published by Kesva an Tavas Kernewek in 1975, the Rev. David R. Evans used *Jowan* for 'John' throughout. Similarly John Page called his translation of the Gospel of St John (Dyllansow Truran 1984) *An Awayl herwyth Sen Jowan* and used that form of the name in his text.

15.2 The name 'Jesus' in Cornish

The Cornish name for 'Jesus' is variously spelt, *ihesu, jhesu, ihesus, iesu.* The form *yesu* is found once only in the toponym *Pontyesu* 'Pantersbridge' in St Neots in 1241. This is a fossilized form which continues *Iesu* < Latin *Iesu,* and is without parallel elsewhere in Cornish. We have seen at 13.8 that etyma with initial *ye-* alternate with forms without the *y, e.g. yethewon* ~ *ethewon* 'Jews'; *yehes* ~ *ehes* 'health' and *yeyn* ~ *eyn* 'cold'. If *ihesu, jhesu, ihesu, iesu* really represented **Yesu,* we would expect to find a variant **Esu.* No such form is attested.

The scribe of BM writes *iesu* 'Jesu' at BM 144, 146. This means he spells the name with the same initial as *ioy* 'joy' BM 4284, 4412, *ienkyn* 'Jenkin' BM 1417, 1449 and *iubyter* 'Jupiter' BM 2327, where the initial ‹i› clearly has the value of English initial *j*.

Lhuyd gives *Dzeziu* under Latin Jesus at AB: 67b. *Dzeziu* looks like a misprint for **Dzheziu*, where the initial segment is *dzh* i.e. [dʒ].

In his translation of Matthew 2 and 4 William Rowe writes the name as *Jesus*. He also writes *Jerman* 'Jeremiah', *Jerusalem* 'Jerusalem', *Jordan* 'Jordan', *Joseph* 'Joseph', *Jowan* 'John' and *Judah* 'Judah'. For him, therefore, all these names begin with initial *J* [dʒ]. There is no reason to believe that Rowe's pronunciation of *Jesus* was significantly different from that of the scribe of BM or of any of the other Middle Cornish texts.

15.3 Further biblical names in *J-*

The following biblical names beginning with *i-*, *j-* and *hi-* are also found in the texts:

iacob 'jacob, james' RD 1007
Jafet 'Japhet' OM 1054; *Japhet* BF: 46, 48
iamys 'James' RD 1375; *jamys* PC 1014, RD 947; *James* ÉCII: 191; *Jamys* TH 48
Jheremy 'Jeremiah' TH 7a x 3; *Jheremye*TH 6a; *Jheremyas* TH 43a
Jerman 'Jeremiah' ÉCII: 199
Jherom 'Jerome' TH 47; *Hierom* TH 49, SA 64
ierusalem 'Jerusalem' PA 29a, 107c, 168c, OM 1928, 1933, 1948, 2060, PC 1649, 2639, *Jherusalem* TH 27a, 47a; *hierusalem* TH 48; *Jerusalem* ÉCII: 193, 194 x 2
Job 'Job' TH 6a, 7, 8
Jonas 'Jonah' TH 45a
Jordan 'Jordan' ÉCII: 190, 193
Iosep 'Joseph' PA 214a, 215a, 215c, 230b, 232a; *iosep* PC 1695, 3139, 3155; *ioseph* RD 3, 22, 31; *Joseph* ÉCII: 198, 200
iosue 'Joshua' OM 1880; *Josue* TH 55a x 3, 55a footnote
jud 'Jude' PC 465; *iude* RD 1031 x 2, 1448
Iudas 'Judas' PA 35d, 36a, 38a, 40a, 47c, 62b, 64a, 64d, 65b, 66a, 103a, 104a, 105c; *iudas* PA 41a, 48a, 106a, 106c, PC 759, 935, 960, 1078, 1101, 1204; *Judas* TH 44a, SA 61 x 2, 65a x 2
Judah 'Judah' ÉCII: 193, 195 x 2
Judeah 'Judea' ÉCII: 194, 195
iudi 'Judea' PC 1594, 1607; *iudy* RD 10
Judith 'Judith' TH 6a.

All these names had initial [dʒ] in traditional Cornish, and should be spelt with ‹J› in the revived language.

CHAPTER 16

Warrant in the texts for *k*, *kw*, *hw*, and *x*

16.1 The textual basis for ‹k› before *a*, o, *u*, *l* and *r*

In some varieties of revived Cornish *k* is written not only before front vowels *e*, *i*, and *y* but also before the back vowels *a*, *o* and *u* and also before *l* and *r*. In order to determine how far such spellings correspond to the practice of the Middle Cornish scribes, I have selected a representative sample of etyma with the relevant features and set out below the attested spellings in them. The texts from which the samples have been taken are all those of the Middle Cornish period, i.e. CF, PA, OM, PC, RD, BM, BK, TH, SA and CW. Later texts have not been used, since the orthography in them is less consistent and in most cases shows only a tentative connection with the Cornish scribal tradition. Lhuyd's orthography is largely phonetic in conception and is therefore indifferent to traditional spelling. Moreover some Late Cornish writers, notably John Boson, imitate some of Lhuyd's orthographic practices. Under each etymon I cite the forms with ‹c› first, and thereafter those instances that exhibit ‹k›.

1) **'bent, wrong'**

cam OM 337, 1126, PC 1403, 2248, 2914, 3034, RD 40, RD 2264, BM 1654, 1770, 2022, 2031, 3755, 3779, 17a, 18, 48a, BK 967, 1474, 2029, 2232, 2829, 2037.

kam CW 804.

2) **'a step, at all'**

cam PA 13a, 85a, PC 1197; *camen* PA 150a; *caman* PA 204a, 205a; *cammen* PC 3126.

kam CF 30.

3) **'hard'**

cales OM 1525, PC 927, 1008, RD 244, 1987, BM 671; *calys* PA 169d, 209d, TH 18, 27a, 53 x 2, BK 3123, 3167; *calis* TH 28.

There are no instances with initial *k*-.

4) **'to love'**

care PA 26b, PC 511, 530, BM 4023; *cara* PA 75b, BM 2567, 4479, TH 9a x 3, 20a x 3, 21, 21a, 22 x 5, 22a x 4, 23, 23a x 7, 24 x 5, 26, 31 x 2, 43 x 6, 54a, BK 395, 2755, CW 669, 699; *a'm care* 'who loved me' PC 1419; *ny's care* 'I do not love them' BM 2044; *me a'th care* 'I love thee' BK

1080; *ny'th cara* 'I do not love you' BK 3184; *y carsen* 'I should like' RD 442, 469, BM 589, 638, 3652.
kara BM 65; *y karsen* 'I should like' BM 15.

5) **'loving, beloved'**
caradow PA 45d, 59b, 64d, 159c, 193c, 218c, OM 679, 721, 1006, 1039, 1114, 1345, 1353, 1625, 2113, 2135, 2757, PC 73, 883, RD 493, 1482, BK 129, 831, 1155, 1714, 2778, 2921; *caradov* BM 833, 1803, 2497, 2902, 3628, 3647; *caradowe* CW 1076.
karadow BM 74.

6) **'to fall'**
cothe PA 22c, 149c, OM 527, 628, TH 16, *cotha* PC 2295, TH 4, 7, 18, 27, 37, 38, 41, 49a x 2; 51; *cothys* 'fallen' OM 1543, 1549, 1569, 1700, 1707, PC 1440, RD 1765, BM 728, 1278; 1310, 1357, 3682, CW 1771; *cothes* 'fallen' TH 3; *bys may cothe* 'until she fall' OM 2718; *cothas* 'fell' RD 1119, 2125, 2334; *ef re cothas* 'he has fallen' PC 2618.

There are no instances with initial *k-*.

7) **'heart'**
colon PA 81d, 101a, 128c, 139a, 141d, 181c, 256c, OM 511, 721, 1264, 1337, 1376, 1381, 1525, 1568, 1608, 1873, PC 2, 24, 32, 539, 1027, 1076, 1147, 1426, 1703, 1743, 1877, 1946, 2610, 2637, 2932, 3164, 3170, 3185, 3224, 3230, RD 456, 483, 503, 695, 700, 707, 724, 748, 760, 1079, 1244, 1250, 1258, 1274, 1322, 1365, 1370, 1367, 1439, 1480, 1523, 1714, 1765, 1801, 1846, 1877, 1896, 2042, 2156, 2241, 2247, 2623, BM 683, 690, 1258, 4102; *colan* BM 1003, TH 9a, 21 x 2, 23a, 30, 54, SA 65a, BK 1702, 2383, 2616, 3026, CW 1964; *colen* OM 428, BM 2049, 3589; *colyn* BM 628, 1804.

There are no instances with initial *k-*.

8) **'body'**
corf PA 35c, 103b, 106c, 130d, 215b, 218c, 230c, 231a, 235b, 241b, 252c, OM 86, 112, 262, 625, 859, 926, 2251, PC 764, 1733, 1753, 2096, 3085, 3100, 3113, 3140, 3183, RD 21, 38, 43, 49, 355, 368, 430, 457, 629, 686, 692, 701, 739, 788, 848, 999, 1035, 1070, 1080, 1115, 1281, 1288, 1301, 1424, 1563, 1657, 1662, 1808, 1839, 2159, 2171, 2180, 2183, 2190, 2216, 2222, 2228, 2273, 2277, 2284, 2310, 2315, 2347, 2570, BM 233, TH 12a, SA 59, 59a x 4, 60, 60a x 2, 61 x 7, 61a x 4, 62 x 5, 62a x 3, 63 x 3, 63a x 5, 64, 64a x 3, 65 x 3, 65a x 5, 66 x 2, 66a x 2, BK 64, 72, 200, 882, 1121, 1272, 1281, 1288, 1452, 1454, 1464, 1603, 1611, 1789, 1916, 1925, 1937, 1945, 1978, 1986, 2877, 2057, CW 394, 873, 1324, 1612, 2081, 2115, 2220; *corff* PA 183b, 227a, 233c, 234c, 235a, BM 523, 711, 1153,

1279, 1611, 1686, 2065, 2404, 2492, 3046, 2052, 3075, 3084, 3139, 3361, 3864, 3956, 4252, 4281, 4300, 4297, 4472, 4527, 4530, 4538, TH 2, 52a, 53a, 54, SA 62a; *corffe* TH 1a, 2, 4 x 2, 11, 12 x 2, 12a, 15a, 31, 42, 52, 53, 53a, 58.

korf BK 2369.

9) **'old'**

coth PA 175c, OM 737, PC 1695, BM 68, TH 6, 6a, 27 x 3, 27a, 49a, SA 59a, CW 1965, 2318; *coyth* OM 855, TH 46; *coith* TH 27, 27a, 28a, 52a.

There are no instances with initial *k*-.

10) **'friend'**

cothman PC 2220, 2431, TH 21a x 2, 22 x 2, 22a, 23a, 25a x 2, CW 764.

There are no instances with initial *k*-.

11) **'speech; to speak, spoken'**

covs PC 1338, 1956, BM 81, 528, 777, 779, 780, 781, 928, 1039, 1050, 1240, 2091, 2120;, 2222, 2964, 3979, 3989, 4046, 4198, 4484; *covse* BM 2360; *cows* PA 81d, 95a, 143c, 165d, 251a, BM 191, TH 7a, 23, 30, 43a, 46, SA 61a, BK 678, 970, 1113, 1288, 1496, 1937, 1945, 2052, 2489; *cowsse* TH 4a, 11a, 18a x 2, 19a, 24a, 44, 48 x 2; *cowse* TH 7a, 9a, 13, 15, 18a x 2, 19a x 2, 22 x 2, 32a, 33, 35, 37, 39a, 41a, 43 x 2, 43a, 44a x 2, 45, 47, 48, 48a x 2, 50a, 53, 54 x 2, 56, 57a, SA 62, 65a, 66, CW 156, 164, 506, 543; *cowsall* CW 557, 2349; *cowsas* PA 89b, SA 61a; *cowsys* BM 180, 229, TH 17a, 32, 43, 44 x 2, 51, 52, 52a, 53 x 2, SA 62a; *cowses* TH 9, CW 828, 1533, 1538.

kowsal BK 15, 626; *kows* BK 1885; *kowse* TH 31; *kowsse* TH 29; *kowses* TH 1; *kowsys* 'spoken' TH 21, 23, 53, BK 2318, 2404, 2436; *kowsyth* BK 1166, 3185; *kowsyn* BK 2168.

12) **'to hide'**

cuthe PA 170b, OM 254, 1924, PC 1370, 1376, RD 538, BM 1736, 1726; *cutha* BM 1025, 1307, CW 1038; *cuthys* OM 866, 1064, 1127, 2438.

kvthe OM 22.

13) **'to shed, to pour'**

scolye PA 36c; *scollye* PC 341; *scollya* BM 1107, 1195, 3504; *scollya'* BK 1459; *scollia* BM 1707; *scollyas* PC 547, BM 1698; *scolyas* BM 131; *scollys* PC 2460, BM 3495, TH 15a; *scollis* TH 11; *scullye* PC 476, 2142; *scullya* CW 2522.

skollia TH 7a; *skulye* PC 260; *skullye* PC 534, 2370; *skullys* PC 825.

14) **'to deny, to reject'**
sconye PA 175d, PC 500; *sconya* CF 11, OM 1238, BM 1754, BK 2028; *sconyas* PA 46a, 174c; *sconyth* PA 120d, *sconyo* OM 2388; *na sconyer* PC 190.

There are no instances with initial *k*-.

15) **'to collect; collection'**
cuntall BK 2109; *cuntell* CW 1293; *contulva* TH 31; *contylles* CW 2322.
kuntel BM 1508, 1515, 1544, 1587, 1877; *kuntullugh* BM 1536; *kuntullys* BM 1560, 1605, 4549; *kuntulys* BM 1779.

16) **'counsel, council; to counsel'**
cusul PC 1915; *cusel* BM 1594, 2141, 3297; *cusyl* OM 1813, 2041, 2267, 2672, 2673, 2802, PC 1005, 1339, 1447, 1453, 1549, 2160, 2481, RD 14, 25, 421, 1130, 1593, 2213, 2222, 2229, BK 968, 978; *cusyll* PA 31c, 116b, TH 28a, 29a, CW 703; *cusullyow* OM 2681, TH 38; *cusyllyow* CW 628; *cusullya* BK 988, 3193a,; *cusyllye* OM 643, PC 567, 1930; *cussylyaf* RD 569; *cussyllyough* PC 1807; *cusullyes* PC 1811; *cusullys* BM 1773; *cusulse* RD 335.
kusyl PC 472; *kusyll* TH 53a; *Kvsell an Nice* 'the Council of Nicaea' SA 65a.

17) **'to sleep; sleep'**
cosca BM 1702, 4189; *coske* PA 51a, 55c, OM 1780, 1905, 1920, 2128, PC 2148, RD 412; *cuske* OM 2047; *cosk* OM 97, 2070; *coske* BM 3770; *coskeugh* PC 1093; *coskyn* RD 402.
koscough PA 61b.

18) **'beloved'**
cuf OM 395, 443, 997, 1873, PC 621, 641, 869, 887, 1877, 3164; *cuff* BM 628, 1003, 1258, 1804, 2049, 4102; *cufyon* PC 1093, BM 2019; *cuvyon* BK 1589, 2058.
kuf PA 256c, OM 285.

19) **'sick, unwell'**
claf OM 1337, 1568, PC 1027, 1426, 2610, 2637, 2677, 2697, RD 724, 775, 1377, 1589, 1664 1847, BK 333, 519, 610, 1096, 2501, 2944; *claff* PA 25c, 155b, 158b,177d, BM 1413, 1853, 3100, 3291, 3312, 3589, 3788, 4520, TH 8a; *claffe* TH 8a; *clave* CW 1199.

There are no instances with initial *k*-.

20) **'hears; hear!'**
clev RD 845; *clew* OM 1389, 1619, 1832, RD 756, 774, 837, 858, 881, 2422; *clow* TH 41a, BK 287, 2774, 2812, 2817, CW 1426, 1580.
klew 'hear' OM 1895.

21) **'strong'**
cref PA 56c, 91b, 122d, 160c, OM 1040, 1490, 1498, 2222, 2451, 2482, PC 276, 1334, 1441, 1858, 2459, 2539, 2631, RD 108, 118, 1569, 1787, 2111, 2135, 2571, BK 406, 806, 2202, 2351, 2698, 3223; *creff* PA 104b, 159b, 209d, 213d, 221d, 226a, 251c, BM 2366, 2155, 3822, 4118, 4145; *cryff* PA 105d, TH 50a; *cryffe* TH 41
kref OM 687, CW 2278.

22) **middle**
cres PA 147b, 186c, OM 1606, 2481, PC 532, RD 2147, TH 3a, 44a, BK 1487, 2646, 3220, 3291.
kres PC 1889, BM 946.

25) **'Christian'**
cristyan BM 939, 2245, TH 20; *christyan* TH 27a; *crystyon* PC 1112, RD 970, 1575; *crystyan* BM 1001, 1111, 1817, 2969; *crystyen* BM 1327, 2517, 1825.
krystyan TH 34a.

27) **'to cry, to call'**
crye OM 1418, PC 2062, 2242, 2249, 2475, 3127, RD 1769, 2304; cryeugh PC 2477; *crya* TH 9a, 40a, BK 25, CW 1270, 1795; *creya* BM 617, 1531, 1816, 2169 , 3620.

There are no instances with initial *k*-.

The overwhelming majority of words are written with *ca-*, *co-*, *cu-*, *cl-*, and *cr-*. Forms like *kows* and *kowsall* have been influenced by forms like *kews* and *kewsel*, where *k* is used regularly before the front vowel. Otherwise the only places where there is any tendency to write *k* are where the consonant is followed by *u* and in particular *un*, e.g., *kuf, kusyl, kuthe, skullye* and *kuntel*. Compare also the spellings *kunda* 'kind' OM 989, 1399; *vnkunda* 'unnatural' TH 30 x 2; *kunys* 'firewood' OM 1296, 1299, 1333, 1387, PC 1219, 1241; *ow kul* 'doing' PC 359, 377 and *ow kull* 'doing' TH 9a, 13, 14a, 15 x 2, 17a, 22, 22a, 30 x 2, 37 x 2, 43, 46, 47, 51a, 52, 53 and 53a. There can be little doubt that ‹ku› and ‹kun› were adopted instead of ‹cu› and ‹cun› by some Cornish scribes when writing in order to avoid the confusion of minims. The collocation ‹cu› was likely to be misread as ‹ai›, and ‹cun› could be mistaken for ‹am› or ‹ani›. Modern writers have no need to fear such confusion and can as unambiguously write ‹cuntel› with initial ‹c›, just like ‹cara› and ‹colon›. Overall a well-designed orthography for revived Cornish should use *c* before all the back vowels (*a, o, u*) and before *l* and *r* as well. Spellings like *kara, konsel, kowethas, kudha, klav* and *kresen* have little to recommend them.

16.2 The use of ‹kw›

In traditional Cornish [kw] is usually written ‹qu›, though the scribe of CW prefers ‹qw›. Here are some attestations from the Middle Cornish texts:

1 **'ever'**

qu/qw: *bythqueth* PA 49c, 84d, 85d, 169c, 223d, PC 384, 522, 916, 1238, 1284, 1295, 1416, 1913, 2034, 2436, 2443, 3135, RD 1659, 1782, 2550, BM 204, 337, 364, 1593, 1868, 2625, 3468, 3596, 3727, 3968, 3973, 4492, TH 11, 15a, 17, 54a; *bytqueth* PA 91d, 172d, 176d, 204b, 214b, OM 2107; *bithquath* TH 59; *bythquath* BK 241, 853, 923, 931, 1208, 1256, 1265, 1682, 1915, 2095; CW 2149, 2340; *bythqwath* 1289, 1393, 1454, 1472, 1739; *bythqwathe* CW 1265; *bysquath* BK 691.

There are no instances with *kw*.

2 **'to show'**

qu/qw: *thysquethaf* OM 1281, RD 1692; *dysquethes* OM 1746; *thysquethes* OM 261; *dysqueȝas* PA 157a; *dysquethas* OM 1439, 2351, TH 13, 23, 42; *thysquethas* TH 35, SA 65a., CW 872; *ymthysquethas* RD 1496; *tysquethas* PA 16b, RD 2637; *tysqueȝas* PA 11b; *dysqueȝyens* PA 236d; *dysque* OM 2106, PC 3229; *thysque* PC 125; *dysquethys* BM 4551, TH 11; *dysquethis* TH 12; *dysquethowgh* BK 2821; *disquetheys* BM 1849; *disquethys* BM 2501; *disquethis* TH 2, 5, 20, SA 60; *disquethas* TH 45a, SA 60 x 2, 63; *thisquethas* TH 31; *tisquethas* SA 61 x 2; *desquethes* TH 26a x 2, 34a, 39a, 51; *desquethis* TH 15a, 16, 21, 30a, 47a x 3, 54a; *dusqua* BK 1234; *dusquethas* BK 2068; *tysqwethas* CW 1873; *thysqwethas* CW 872.

There are no instances with *kw*.

4 **'if you do'**

qu/qw: *mar qureth* OM 1284, BM 903, 1218, 1701, 2561, 2580, 4012, BK 582, 629; *mar qureta* BK 50; *mar que(r)th* RD 921; *mara qureth* OM 1495, PC 845, 1772, 1901; *mar qwreth* CW 220, 513 (variant), 619 (variant), 667 (variant); *mar qwreta* CW 488 (variant), 738 (variant); *mara qwrees* CW 577.

There are no instances with *kw*.

5 **'quick'**

qu/qw: *quyk* OM 1406, 1530, PC 2828, RD 1731, BM 2481; *quik* BM 827, 943, 1092, 1231, 1334 , 1552, 1794, 2089, 2410, 3229, 3791, 4142; *quyck* C 1468, 1567; *quick* BK 34, CW 2412; *quicke* CW 1208; *qwyck* CW 2112; *qwicke* CW 2383 (variant).

There are no instances with *kw.*

6 **'to require'**

qu: *requyrye* PC 2474; *requyria* TH 24a, 27; *requyrya* TH 24a, 26a, CW 2520; *requyrys* TH 16a, 28; 51a; *requyris* TH 28; *requiria* TH 16, 27, 30, 51.

There are no instances with *kw.*

7 **'tired'**

squ/sqw: *squyth* PA 132a, OM 684, 1009, 2049, 2824, PC 2509, RD 846, BM 1685, BK 1026, CW 1730, 1792; *squeth* BM 633; *squeyth* OM 2699; *sqwyth* CW 2001.

There are no instances with *skw.*

8 **'to hit, to break'**

squ: *squattis* BM 3053, CW 1705; *squatyes* CW 1707; *squat* CW 2282.

There are no instances with *skw.*

9 **'to tear'**

squ: *squerdye* RD 490, 1283; *squerdya* BM 3914; *squerdyas* PA 94b, 106c; *squerdys* PC 2848, 3172, 3178, RD 1266, BM 4191; *squerdis* BM 1281; *squardye* PA 195d; *squardyas* PA 209c; *squardis* PA 181d, SA 60; *squardijs* PA 133c, 135b; *squard* PA 166c.

There are no instances with *skw.*

In Middle Cornish there seems to be only one example of ‹kw› in the phrase *war skwych* 'with a jerk' at PC 2595. There is also two examples of ‹sku› in: *gesough hy a bart malan yn morter skuat the gothe* 'let it fall with a bang into the mortise' PC 2815-16 and *skuerdye* 'to tear PC 2845. Otherwise the scribes of Middle Cornish used ‹qu› and ‹squ›, although William Jordan, the scribe of CW used ‹qw› and ‹sqw› on occasion. An authentic orthography for revived Cornish would use ‹qu› or ‹qw› and ‹squ› and ‹sqw›. There is no justification for ‹kw› or ‹skw›.

16.3 *k* immediately before *n*

Middle Cornish seems to have had no difficulty with the initial cluster *kn-*, for example in *knoukye* 'to knock, to strike' OM 2676, 2694, 2699, PC 2077, RD 1893 and *knak oma* 'on the spot' BM 1644, 1652. In Modern English, however, the cluster [kn] is unknown, since the initial *k* is now lost. English speakers can pronounce *k* followed by *n* only by inserting a furtive schwa between the two sounds. This can be seen, for example, in the way that the English refer to the Danish king of England as *Canute*, whereas the Danes call him *Knut*.

Although there is no evidence that the first element in the initial cluster *kn-* was being lost in Cornish, it does seem that a furtive schwas was inserted between the two segments. The Cornish for 'nut' was originally *knofen* f., with a collective plural **know*; cf. Welsh *cneuen* 'nut', coll. *cnau*. Lhuyd, however, cites the following:

> *Kynyfan* 'A nut'AB: 101c; *Kynyphan* 'A Nut' AB: 8c; *Kynyphan frenk* 'A Wall-nut' AB:, 74a.

It seems that in the spoken Cornish of Lhuyd's day schwa had been added between the first and the second segment of the word. The same phenomenon is to be seen also in *Dho kyniviaz* glossing *Tondeo* 'to clip or shear' AB: 164bc. This contrasts with *knevys* 'sheared' TH 23. A furtive schwa is also apparent in Lhuyd's *kynava* 'a knave, rascal, rogue' AB: 97c s.v. *Nebulo*. This contrasts with *knava* TH 28a x 2.

16.4 The collocation ‹hw›

The Old Cornish Vocabulary writes voiceless *w* as *hƿ*, that is, *h* followed by wynn ‹ƿ› in conformity with Anglo-Saxon scribal practice, as the letter ‹w› did not exist then. Lhuyd in his phonetic system writes voiceless *w* as ‹hu›, often with a dot under the *u*, e.g. *huî*/*hụî* 'you', *huêl*/*hụêl* 'work', *huâth*/*hụâth* 'yet', etc. In traditional Cornish, however, voiceless *w* is usually written ‹wh›, although it is sometimes written ‹w›, presumably to indicate that devoicing has been lost. There is no example anywhere in traditional Cornish of ‹hw› to represent voiceless *w*. The revived language is by its nature a construct, and one which some will always consider less than authentic. There is no need therefore to introduce into its orthography a graph that is both unnecessary and alien to traditional practice. The use of ‹hw› in such words as *hwarvos* 'to happen', *hwath* 'still', *hweg* 'sweet, dear', *hwedhel* 'story', *hwegh* 'six', *hwesa* 'to perspire', *hwetha* 'to blow', *y hwrug* 'did' divorces the written language from that written by Cornishmen when the language was still spoken. Worse still it gives Cornish an artificial appearance and for nor coherent reason. It has moreover been pointed out that ‹hw› can mislead speakers to pronounce the segment as [hw] or [xw], neither of which is warranted by the attested orthography. The spelling ‹wh› shows that the intended pronunciation is [ʍ] and speakers who fail to pronounce it thus and substitute [w] are in any event doing nothing that is not attested in traditional Cornish. The adoption of ‹Hw› and ‹hw› into spelling of the revived language was a serious mistake and needs to be remedied as soon as possible. ‹Hw› and ‹hw› should be replaced immediately by ‹Wh› and ‹wh›.

16.5 The use of ‹x› in Cornish

The letter ‹x› is not uncommon in traditional Cornish orthography. Here are a few examples:

box 'box' (receptacle) PA 35a, 36b, PC 485
box 'box, blow' PA 81b, 1269; *boxow* pl. PA 120d
**boxas* 'box, blow'; pl. *boxsesow* PC 1362, 1367; *boxsusow* PC 1389
boxusy 'to box, to strike' PC 1274
exilyys 'exiled' OM 1576
exaltya 'to exalt' BM 15, 2798; *exaltye* BM 18, 2900; *exaltia* TH 8, 10; *exaltijs* 'exalted' BM 2942; *exaltys* 'exalted' CW 229, 310, 446, 651, 701
examnya 'to examine' TH 23a, CW 301; *examnye* PC 1451, 1467, 2149, 2176; *examne* PC 1210
exampyll 'example' TH 5; *exampil* TH 6; *exampill* TH 6a, 21a, 39; *examplys* pl. TH 10; *examplis* pl. TH 25a; *examples* pl. TH 23, 56a; *exampels* pl. SA 61a
text 'text' TH 26a, 37a, 42
vexia 'to vex, to annoy' TH 22; *vexijs* 'vexed' BM 2630.

Some orthographies for Cornish dispense with ‹x› and write ‹ks› instead. This is most unfortunate. In English when *x* comes after a stressed vowel it is pronounced [ks], e.g. *box, text, vexya.* When however it precedes a stressed vowel it is voiced to [gz], for example in *exalt, examine.* It is probable that speakers of revived Cornish will similarly pronounce ‹x› in *exaltya, examnya,* etc. with voicing. If so the spelling **eksaltya,* **eksamnya* does not reflect their pronunciation. It would be more sensible to leave ‹x› in such words and thus leave open the question of whether the segment is voiced or unvoiced.

The same problem incidentally is apparent in the spelling of *possessyon* 'possession' which is clearly borrowed from English. If this is spelt ‹possessyon› in Cornish ‹ss› in both cases is pronounced [s]. In English, however, the first cluster is pronounced [z], because it comes immediately before the accent. It seems likely that users of revived Cornish will pronounce the word with [z] for the first ‹ss› also. In which case, *possessyon* should be written ‹posessyon› to allow for voicing of *-ss-* before the accent.

CHAPTER 17

Days of the week and festivals

In some orthographies for revived Cornish the names of the days of the week and feast days are spelt with initial ‹dy'› or ‹de'›, e.g. *dy'Lun, de'Lun* 'Monday', *de'Yow, dy'Yow* as though the first element were *dydh* or *dedh* 'day', but with an elided final segment. This is a serious mistake and shows that the devisers of the orthographies were unaware of the history of the forms in question.

The word for 'day' is *dydd* 'in Welsh, *dyth* or *deth* in traditional Cornish, and *deiz* in Breton. This forms are reflexes of IE **diyews*, where the medial *-iy-* resulted in the voiced dental fricative seen at the end of the Brythonic etyma. In the adverbial forms, however, the first element is the reflex of an the oblique stem, for example, the IE genitive **diwés* or **diwós*. In these forms there was no medial collocation *-iy-* and thus no Brythonic [ð] deriving from it. The absence of any final [ð] can be seen in the following Middle Welsh forms: *dyw Awst* 'Lammas', *dyw Calan* 'New Year's Day', *Dyw Gwener y Groglith* 'Good Friday', *dyw Gŵyl Mihangel* 'Michaelmas', *dyw Gŵyl Ystwyll* 'Epiphany', etc. The absence of the voiced final dental fricative is also apparent in the attested Cornish forms:

Dezil 'Sunday' AB: 54c; *Dewsull blegyow* 'Palm Sunday' PA 27a
De lîn 'Monday' AB: 54c
De merh 'Tuesday' AB: 14c
dumerher 'Wednesday' BM 2254; *De marhar* 'Wednesday' AB: 54c
deyow 'Thursday' BM 3159; *deyow hablys* 'Maundy Thursday' PA 41c; *duyow hamlos* 'Maundy Thursday' PC 654; *deow habblys* 'Maundy Thursday' SA 66
dugwener 'Friday' BM 120; *Du guener* 'Friday' BM 4316; *du guener* 'Friday' BM 4318, 4321, 4420; *De guenar* 'Friday' AB: 54c
De Zadarn 'Saturday' AB: 54c
du fencost myttyn 'on the morning of Pentecost' TH 44a
du Halan an vlethan 'New Year's Day' BK 1880-81
Degl stûl 'Epiphany' AB 57a
dugol myhal 'Michaelmas' BM 2076; *dugol myhall* 'Michaelmas' BM 2201
du pask vyttyn 'on Easter morning' RD 1108
dew whallon gwa 'All Saints' Day' Wakelin: 89.

It is clear that in the native Cornish forms for the days of the week and festivals the initial formant was *de, du* or *dew* without any sign of a final dental. Against this one must cite the form *deth yov* 'Thursday' at BM 1472, where the scribe has inserted *th*. This is at variance with his *deyow* at BM 3159, his five examples of *dugwener, duguener* 'Friday', his *dumerher* 'Wednesday' and his two examples of *dugol* is his name for 'Michaelmas'. *Deth yov* is to be explained as a form by hypercorrection, and is itself ahistorical. Equally mistaken is John Boson's *De'Zîl* 'the Sabbath Day' BF: 55, where the apostrophe is unnecessary, since nothing has been omitted or elided.

Two points must to be stressed here. In the first place there is no historical justification for writing *Dy'* or *De'* before the days of week in revived Cornish. The initial element never had a final consonant and to insert an apostrophe to indicate its omission is an error. Secondly the vowel of the formant in traditional Cornish is written ‹e›, ‹u›, or ‹ew›. There is no instance of **Dy-* anywhere in traditional Cornish. The revived language should write either *Du-* [dɪw] or *De-*. Anything else is inauthentic.

CHAPTER 18

Problems with the Standard Written Form (SWF)

18.1 An orthography devised without academic input

The Standard Written Form (originally the Single Written Form) is the officially promoted orthography for revived Cornish. Unfortunately it was devised by a committee of revivalists with a minimum of input from linguistic experts. Indeed experts were deliberately excluded from the process. Not astonishingly the SWF is very imperfect and until it is radically revised is unlikely to gain academic approval.

Apart from the two matters of etymological spellings and the supposed distinction between Middle Cornish *lyver, tyller* and Late Cornish *lever, teller,* I deal below exclusively with problems in the consonantal system of the SWF. The errors and inconsistencies in the vowels and diphthongs of the SWF are many, but they will have to be left to a later date.

18.2 Variants in the SWF

One of the most bizarre aspects of the Standard Written Form is that it prescribes what are known as Main Forms, alongside so-called Traditional Forms. The Main Forms are words spelt with the three graphs ‹hw›, ‹k› before back vowels, *l,* and *r,* and ‹kw›. Traditional Forms on the other hand are words written with ‹wh›, ‹c›, and ‹qw›. Thus the Main Forms *hweg* 'sweet, dear', *klewes* 'to hear' and *skwith* 'tired' when written as Traditional Forms will be *wheg, clewes* and *sqwith* respectively. There is thus no difficulty in converting from one set to the other. There is, however, a much more serious question. Those using the official orthography for Cornish acknowledge that one group of spellings are "traditional" and the others, though not traditional, are "Main Forms" and so to be promoted in preference to the others. In this way by their very terminology the proponents of the SWF are declaring that their default variants are not traditional and are *ipso facto* inauthentic. Cornish as the resuscitated form of a once extinct language has always been open to criticism of being less than completely genuine (see, for example, Price 1992). If those who devised the SWF are prepared publicly to acknowledge that their preferred variants, the Main Forms, are not traditional, then any claim revived Cornish may have to authenticity is fatally compromised. People who are less than favourably disposed to the Cornish Revival in the first place, when learning of the distinction made between "Main" and "Traditional" forms, may well conclude that "Main Form" Cornish is intrinsically inauthentic and does not therefore merit any public funding.

We have seen at 16.1 and 16.2 that ‹k› before *l* and *r* and back vowels, and ‹kw› are at best marginal in the orthography of traditional Cornish. We have also noted that there is no warrant at all for the graph ‹hw› in the traditional language. The obvious conclusion is that the so-called Main Form graphs are indefensible and should be replaced with the traditional ones.

18.3 Etymological spellings

The Standard Written Form writes *bryntin* 'grand, noble', *kegin* 'kitchen', *Latin* 'Latin', *melin* 'mill', and *myttin* 'morning'. As has been noted at 14.1 above, nowhere in Middle Cornish is the final unstressed syllable written ‹in› in any of these etyma. The unstressed syllable is pronounced [ɪn] in every case and is spelt either ‹yn› or ‹en›. To attempt to distinguish in writing the unstressed syllable in *bryntin, kegin, myttin,* for example, from that in *lemmyn* 'now', *termyn* 'time', and *tokyn* 'sign, token' is unjustified and introduces an unnecessary complication into the orthography. These five etyma in any official orthography ought to be spelt *bryntyn, kegyn, Latyn, melyn* and *myttyn,* exactly as they were spelt by Nance in Unified Cornish. This point in the SWF should be emended.

18.4 "Middle Cornish" versus "Late Cornish" variants

The SWF allows specifically "Late" variants on the grounds that Late Cornish was radically distinct from Middle Cornish and that the differences should be given recognition in the orthography. Such an opinion is largely unfounded and indeed was disputed by Jenner himself, who believed, correctly in my view, that the differences between Middle and Late Cornish were small.

One alleged difference between Middle and Late Cornish is the stressed short vowel in such words as *lyver* 'book' and *tyller* 'place'. The SWF specifies *lyver* as Middle Cornish and *lever* as Late Cornish. Similarly *tyller* is thought to be Middle Cornish and *teller* is the Late variant. None of this is true since *lever* 'book' is commoner in Middle Cornish than *lyver* and *teller* is as common in Middle Cornish as *tyller*. *Lyver* and *lever, tyller* and *teller,* etc. should be allowed in any well-constructed orthography for Cornish, but to label one Middle Cornish and the other Late is mistaken.

18.5 Voiced and voiceless final consonants in the SWF

The SWF writes *carrek* 'rock' but *wheg* 'sweet, dear', *medhek* 'doctour' but *gwag* 'empty, hungry', *gorthyp* 'answer' but *mab* 'son', *morrep* 'seashore' but *heb* 'without'. The SWF also writes *imach* 'image, statue' and *ertach* 'heritage' and thus devoices the final segment in these borrowings from English. Thereafter the orthography ignores the voice ~ voiceless rule and uses the voiced consonants after both stressed and unstressed vowels. Thus the SWF writes *bedh* 'grave' and *gwragedh* 'wives', *coodh* 'falls' and *kerydh* 'thou lovest', *sav* 'stand!' and *gwelav* 'I see', *cov* 'memory' and *genev* 'with me'. To be fair the SWF is merely following Jenner in this matter, who writes in his *Handbook* of 1904, *ragov* 'for me', *orthev* 'upon me', *genev* 'with me,' *bedhav* 'I shall be', *carav* 'I love', *eledh* 'angels', *gwrêgedh* 'wives' and *abesteledh* 'apostles'. In all these Jenner follows

Lhuyd. Unlike the SWF, however, Jenner does write *gwiryoneth* 'truth' not **gwiryonedh*.

As we have seen in Chapters 3 and 4, in all the above cases the unstressed syllable is followed by a voiceless final segment. The SWF here, more than anywhere needs to be revised. It should write *gwrageth* 'wives', *keryth* 'thou lovest', *gwelaf* 'I see', and *genef* 'with me'. Since this is such an important matter I intend to deal with it at length here:

18.5.1 Final *-dh* in the SWF > *-th*

'lord'

arloth OM 105. Lhuyd under *Dominus* 'lord' gives *Arleth* and †*arluydh* AB: 55b. The second of these has an obelus before it, which suggests it is Old Cornish. In OCV 188, however, the word is given an *arluit*, which means that Lhuyd has respelt it in conformity with *arglwydd* 'lord' in his native Welsh. His *Arleth* is probably what he heard in Cornwall and has a voiceless final segment as is to be expected after an unstressed vowel. *Arleth* is a common spelling in Late Cornish; e.g. ÉCII: 174, 178 x 2, 183, etc. SWF **arlodh* > *arloth*.

'wish'

bolungeth OM 873. This word has nothing to do with Welsh *bodlonedd* 'contentment'. It seems rather to have been borrowed into Cornish from Middle Breton *bolontez*, itself a borrowing from French *volonté* < Latin *voluntat(em)*. The word in Breton has been assimilated to native words ending in *-ez* (cf. MB *guirionnez* 'truth'). In Cornish the word may orignally have ended in *-edh*, but the final segment has been devoiced by the Prosodic Shift. It is often written with metathesis and is sometimes simplified. I have collected the following examples: *bolungeth* OM 873, 1277; *volungeth* OM 1165, 1271, 1320, 1329, 1376, PC 2053, RD 745, *bolnegeth* BM 310, 321, 348; *volnogeth* OM 2352, BM 1740; 4340; *volnegeth* PC 957, 1072, BM 1909; *blonogeth* TH 1, 12, 16, 18, 22a, 50, 50a x 3; *blonogath* TH 1a, 4a, 12a, 13a, 14a, 21a, 22, 22a x 5, 23, 23a x 2, 40a, 47a, 49a, SA 60, CW 96; *bolenegoth* PC 1139; *voluneth* OM 1292; *bonogath* BF: 27, 45. Lhuyd writes *Bolenegeth* (AB: 240c) and includes the word with *Skiantoleth* 'Prudence', *Folneth* 'Folly', *Myhterneth* 'Sovereignty', *Kyzaleth* 'Peace', and *Gouegneth* 'Fraud, deceit', all of which have a voiceless final. There is little doubt therefore that this etymon should be written with final *-eth*. SWF **bolonjedh* > *bolonjeth*.

'truth'

guyryoneth PC 595, *guyroneth* OM 702, *gwryoneth* TH 10. Lhuyd gives †*Guirionedh* at AB: 171c, and the dagger implies that he did not actually hear the word; the final segment is by analogy with Welsh *gwirionedd*.

Lhuyd also cites *gwyroneth* at AB: 240c. Jenner gives *gwiryoneth* (*Handbook*: 76) as one of a list of abstract nouns in *-eth*. Since the final syllable is unstressed, we expect the final segment to be voiceless. SWF **gwiryonedh > gwiryoneth.*

'mountain'

meneth PA 16a, *mene'* BK 1161. Lhuyd is led astray by his native Welsh and respells Old Cornish *menit* 'mons' OCV 717 as †*menydh* AB: 93c, 259a. He also gives *Monedh brâz* AB: 93c and *Moneth brâz* s.v. *Mons* at AB: 295a. The stressed vowel ‹o› is suspicious and may have been suggested by the Latin *Mons*. One of Lhuyd's examples, however, *Moneth brâz*, has a voiceless final segment in the word for 'mountain'. Lhuyd has not been influenced by his native Welsh here and the final segment of *Moneth* may be genuine. Lhuyd gives *Menedh* and *mener* for 'mountain' AB: 250c and on the next page he says: '*I find* dh *in the Termination sometimes changed into* r; *As* †Menedh *A mountain, now* mener' AB: 231a. It seems then that Lhuyd did not actually hear *menedh* with a final voiced segment, but rather *mener*. The voiced final in Lhuyd's †*menedh* as in his †*menydh* has been provoked by Welsh *mynydd* 'mountain'. Both *menna* and *mener* are attested in place-names (CPNE: 163). The development *meneth > mener* is perplexing, but it is probably correct to assume first, that the final *r* was voiceless and second, was perhaps substituted for a weakening *-th* in order to maintain the disyllabic nature of the word. Note that the voiced segment reappears in the plural *meneth*, but *menydhyow*. SWF **menedh > meneth*

'new'

nowyth PA 107d, 109c; *noweth* TH 31, SA 66. Lhuyd gives *neuydh* AB: 100c. In the story of "Jowan Chy an Hordh", however, he writes *an vòr noueth* at §6 and *an vòr noueꝛ* at §16 (AB: 251a, 252a). Lhuyd's *neuydh* was clearly suggested by Welsh *newydd*. His two instances of *noueth* with a voiceless final were probably taken down from dictation and are therefore more likely to be genuine. In its original form 'new' in the SWF was *nowyth*. This should replace *nowydh*, the preferred form at present. SWF **nowydh > nowyth*.

18.5.1.1 *th* and *dh* in plurals and duals

Following the rule that original unstressed *-edh* is devoiced as a result of the Prosodic Shift an appears in Middle Cornish as *-eth* (later *-ath* and *-a*) any plural ending in original *-edh* became *-eth* in Middle Cornish and should be so written. In which case the following should be emended in the SWF:

'apostles'
abesteleth RD 813, 1469, BM 4559; *abosteleth* TH 18a, 19, 33, etc.; *apostelath* SA 64a. SWF **abosteledh* > *abosteleth*

'shepherds, herdsmen'
beguleth TH 42; *bugula* TH 33a, *bugolath* BK 742. SWF **buguledh* > *buguleth*

'brotherhood, brethren'
bredereth PC 714, BM 1755, 4252; *brodereth* TH 42a; *broderath* ÉCII: 191. SWF **brederedh* > *bredereth*

'angels'
eleth PA 14b, 18d, OM 10, 586; *elath* SA 59, 60a. SWF **eledh* > *eleth*

'wives'
gvraget OM 975. SWF **gwragedh* > *gwrageth*

'kings'
myghterneth RD 712, *myterneth* BM 2428, TH 6a, 50a; *maternath* SA 62; *vyterneth* BM 2430. SWF **myghternedh* > *myghterneth, myterneth.*

'sisters'
The plural is not attested. SWF **wherydh* > *wheryth*

Prontereth 'priesthood' is already spelt with a final -th in the SWF.

The word for 'shoulder' in the SWF is *scoodh*. The permitted duals are either *diwscodh* or *dewscodh*. Since the dual is stressed on the first syllable, the second is unstressed and thus the final segment is voiceless and should be written ‹th›. SWF **diwscodh* / **dewscodh* > **diwscoth* / *dewscoth*. (Ideally the dual with a feminine form of *dew* should be spelt *dywscoth* rather than as unattested *diwscoth*; cf. *agas dywscoth* 'your shoulders' PC 3068.)

18.5.1.2 Final *dh* > *th* in compounds

The medial segment ‹th› in *ysethe, setha* 'to sit' is voiced [ð]. In the 3rd person singular of the present-future and second person imperative, however, the segment occurs finally after an unstressed syllable in *yseth* 'sits' PA 244d, *eseth* 'sit!' BM 2462. The same root occurs in the word *gorseth*, which has been borrowed from Welsh *gorsedd*. In the Cornish word, because the second syllable is unstressed, the final segment is [θ] not [ð], i.e. ['gorsəθ]. Consequently the word should be spelt ‹gorseth› as, for example, in *Gorseth Kernow*. The document *The Ceremonies of the Gorsedd of the Bards of Cornwall* was a few years ago converted from Unified Cornish spelling to the SWF. On the cover of the booklet the Gorsedd is called *Gorsedh Berdh Kernow*, but the title in the arms above remains *Gorseth Kernow*.

18.5.2 Final *v* > *f*

As has been pointed out at 4.4–4.5 above the final segment in the first person present-future of disyllabic and polysyllabic verbs should be *f* not *v*. Here are some examples of the essential emendations:

v > *f* in the first person singular of verbs

'I shall be'; cf. *y fethaff* BM 1101; *bethaf* OM 2111. SWF **bydhav* > *bedhaf*
'I shall live'; cf. *mar pewaff* BM 1864. SWF **bewav* > *bewaf*
'I love'; cf. *y'th caraf* PC 710; *caraff* TH 43. SWF **carav* > *caraf*
'I hear'; cf. *a glewaf* OM 587; *a glowaf* CW 1166. SWF **clewav*, **clowav* > *clewaf*, *clowaf*
'I command'; cf. *y comondyaff* BM 1862, 3293. SWF **comondyav* > *comondyaf*
'I call, I cry'; cf. *creyaff* BM 1047. SWF **criav*, **creiav* > *criaf*, *creiaf*
'I shall send'; cf. *a thanvonaf* RD 1176. SWF **danvonav* > *danvonaf*
'I am'; cf. *eth esoff* TH 17; *yth esaf* PC 1224. SWF **esov* > *esof*
'I can'; cf. *ny allaff* PA 156d; *ny allaf* OM 946. SWF **gallav* > *gallaf*
'I shall leave'; cf. *gasaf* RD 1584. SWF **gasav* > *gasaf*
'I grant'; cf. *a wrontyaf* OM 74. SWF **grontyav* > *grontyaf*
'I shall warn'; cf. *ny'n guarnyaf* PC 1968. SWF **gwarnyav* > *gwarnyaf*
'I say'; cf. *lauaraff* PA 8; *ny lauaraf* OM 179. SWF **lavarav* > *lavaraf*
'I shall meet'; *pur in metyaff* BM 4186. SWF **metyav* > *metyaf*
'I shall see'; *pan welaff* PA 166d; *ny welaf* OM 588, RD 1962. SWF **gwelav* > *gwelaf*
'I seek'; cf. *ny whelaff ve* TH 22a. SWF **whilav* > **whilaf*
'I thank'; cf. *in grassaff* BM 1858; *y grassaf* RD 508. SWF **grassav* > *grassaf*
'I shall wash'; cf. *nyth wolhaff* PA 46c, *nyth wolhaf* PC 857. SWF **golghav* > *golhaf*
'I shall deny'; cf. *nyth nahaff* PA 49d; *na nahaf* OM 2655. SWF **naghav* > *nahaf*
'I shall write'; cf. *ny scrifaf* PC 2805. SWF **scrifav* > *scrifaf*
'I shall spare'; cf. *ny sparyaf* PC 1788, 2187. SWF **sparyav* > *sparyaf*
'I shall delay'; cf. *ny strechyaff* PA 158c; *ny strechyaf* RD 1625. SWF **strechyav* > *strechyaf*.

v > *f* in prepositional pronouns

'of me'; cf. *ahanaff* PA 193b; *ahanaf* OM 520, 2206, PC 892; *ahaneff* BM 3380. SWF **ahanav* > *ahanaf*

'from me'; cf. *theworthef* OM 206; *thyworthyf* OM 503, 2131; *theworthaf* OM 617; *the ortheff* BM 2577, 2658. SWF **a-dhyworthiv* > *adhyworthyf* 'through me'; cf. *drethof* OM 135; *drethaf* CW 228, 465, 1573, 1989. SWF **dredhov* > *dredhof.*

'before me'; cf. *athyragof* OM 1955, PC 196. SWF *dheragov* > *dheragof*

'with me'; cf. *geneff* PA 63c, BM 492; *genef* OM 417, 739; *gynef* PC 258; *genaf* OM 672. SWF **genev* > *genef*

'upon, to me'; cf. *orthyf* OM 150; *worthyf* PC 1113; *ortheff* BM 407; *orthaf* CW 232; *worthaf* CW 1619. SWF **orthiv, *worthiv* > *orthyf, worthyf*

'for me'; cf. *ragoff* PA 168d, BM 1849; *ragof* OM 139, PC 3137; *ragaf* BK 2828. SWF **ragov* > *ragof.*

The attested forms *theworthef, theworthaf, the ortheff* and *ortheff, orthaf, worthaf* indicate just how unsuitable is the collocation **-iv* in *dheworthiv* and *worthiv* in the SWF. It is difficult to see why **-iv* was adopted in such cases.

18.5.2.1 Final *v* > *f* in compounds

The expression *saf yn ban* 'get up, stand up' is attested at OM 65, PC 2240 and *na saf yn ban* 'do not get up' occurs at OM 97. A reduced form *sa'ban* occurs at OM 933, OM 3711 and BK 4. We can be sure that the final segment in *saf* was voiced, since the phrase appears as *save in ban* at CW 351 and as *save aman* at ÉCII: 198.

The modern neologism for 'station' has been borrowed from Welsh *gorsaf* (cf. Breton *arsav* 'gare, station'). Although the second syllable is from the same root as *saf*/ *save,* it is unstressed. The word therefore ought to appear as *gorsaf.* SWF **gorsav* > *gorsaf.*

18.5.2.2 *f* before *r*

For 'books' the SWF allows *levrow* and *lyvrow*. As we have seen at 9.1 above *lefrow, lyfrow* and *lyfryow* should also be allowed.

For 'to free, to deliver' the SWF gives *delivra,* where ‹i› rather than ‹y› is unmotivated. As is clear from 9.1 *delyfra* should also be allowed.

The SWF gives *nevra* 'never' only. As is clear from 9.2 above, this is a later form of *nefra* (also spelt *neffra*). *Nefra* ought to be allowed in the SWF also.

The SWF gives *yn tevri* 'indeed' only. As is clear from 9.3 above this is a later form of *yn tefry,* (also *yn teffry*) which ought to be sanctioned in the SWF also.

18.5.2.3 'to get'

The SWF allows *cavos* (cf. MB *kavout*) and *cawas,* but these are variants of the same word. A form with intervocalic [f] is also attested (cf. MB *caffout*). Some examples are listed at 5.1.1 above; see also GG 179-81). The SWF should allow *cafos.*

18.6 The distribution of *gh* ~ *h*

Jenner wrote singular *flogh* but plural *flehes*. Nance on the other hand used *-gh-* in both cases. We have seen at 12.1-12.3 above that *gh* represents [x] and occurs at the end of a syllable; intervocalically, however, the authentic sound is *h* [h] not *gh* [x]. At present the SWF follows Nance. In the interest of authenticity, however, it should imitate Jenner. This will mean the following emendations:

SWF **a-ughov* 'above me' > *a-uhof*
SWF **boghow* 'cheeks' > *bohow* (but *bogh*)
SW **fleghes* 'children > *flehes* (but *flogh*)
SWF **seghes* 'drought, thirst' > *sehes* (but *segh*)
SWF **yeghes* 'health' > *yehes* (but *yagh*)

Similarly *-lgh-* and *rgh-* when the *l* or *r* and *gh* are in different syllables, should be written as ‹lh› and ‹rh› respectively:

SWF **golghi* > *golhi* (but *golgh*)
SWF **helghi* > *helhi* (but *helgh*)
SWF **arghans* 'silver' > *arhans*
SW **kerghes* 'to fetch' > *kerhes* (but *kergh*)
SWF **marghek* 'horseman' > *marhek*
SWF **myrghes* 'daughters' > *myrhes* (but *myrgh*).

The SWF already writes *gorhel* for 'ship', not **gorghel*.

18.6.1 The Cornish for 'small'

For 'small' the SWF gives *byghan* and *bian* as a Late form. **Byghan* is unattested in the Cornish texts, although PA has *beghan* at PA 53c and 166b. *Byen, byan* is by far the commonest form in Middle Cornish, although *byhan* does occur. SWF **byghan* > *byhan* and *bian*.

18.6.2 The Cornish for 'king'

For 'king' the SWF gives *myghtern; metern* is allowed as a Late variant. It is very difficult, however, for some learners to pronounce [xt] at the end of an unstressed syllable. Perhaps it might be sensible for the SWF also to allow *mytern* for the Middle Cornish form, which is as old as *Beunans Meriasek* (1504).

18.7 'Need, necessity'

In the SWF 'need, necessity' is either *edhom* or *odhom*. As we have seen at 3.2 there is no evidence for a voiced medial segment here. *Edhom, odhom* should be replaced by *ethom* and *othem*.

18.8 Pre-occlusion and absence of pre-occlusion

Some nouns pre-occlude their final *nn* or *m* after a short vowel while others do not. The SWF, however, does not distinguish between the two classes. We thus find in the SWF the following:

A
gonn 'I know' which does not pre-occlude.
B
bronn 'breast' and *brodn* with pre-occlusion.
gonn 'gun' and *godn* with pre-occlusion.
lonn 'bullock' and *lodn* with pre-occlusion.

A
mann 'zero, naught' which does not pre-occlude.
B
glann 'bank' and *gladn* with pre-occlusion.
gwann 'weak' and *gwadn* with pre-occlusion
splann 'bright, gleaming' and *spladn* with pre-occlusion.

A
jynn 'engine, device' which does not pre-occlude.
B
gwynn 'white' and *gwydn* with pre-occlusion.
lynn 'lake' and *lydn* with pre-occlusion.
tynn 'sharp, painful' and *tydn* with pre-occlusion.

A
namm 'spot, stain' which does not pre-occlude.
B
camm 'bent, crooked' and *cabm* with pre-occlusion.
lamm 'jump, leap', and *labm* with pre-occlusion.
tamm 'scrap', and *tabm* with pre-occlusion.

The SWF should devise a way of distinguishing in writing the words in A above from those in B. Some write *gòn, màn, jyn, nàm* alongside *brodn/bronn, godn/gonn, lodn/lonn, gladn/glann, gwadn/gwann, spladn/splann, gwydn/gwynn, lydn/lynn, tydn/tynn, cabm/camm, labm/lamm,* and *tabm/tamm.*

18.9 Biblical names beginning with *J*

In some Cornish versions of the Holy Scriptures personal names and place-names beginning with *J* in English are spelt with *Y*, e.g. **Yesu, *Yakob, *Yason, *Yesse, *Yoanna, *Yosafat, *Yosep* and **Yosef, *Yowann, *Yudas, *Yunias, *Yustus, *Yeriko, *Yerusalem, *Yoppa* and **Yudi*. In these versions *James,* however, is always *Jamys* (for this question, see Williams (2007)). As we have seen above, there is no justification for such names in *Y*. They should all be spelt with *J* and in any official translation or official list of names this spelling should be made clear.

18.10 The days of the week and festivals

In the SWF 'feast-day, holiday' is **dy'gol, de'gol*. The days of the week in the SWF are as follows: *dy'Sul* and *de'Sul* 'Sunday'; *dy'Lun* and *de'Lun* 'Monday'; *dy'Meurth* and *de'Meurth* 'Tuesday'; *dy'Mergher* and *de'Merher* 'Wednesday'; *dy'Yow* and *de'Yow* 'Thursday'; *dy'Gwener* and *de'Gwener* 'Friday' and *dy'Sadorn* and *de'Sadorn* 'Saturday'. The distinction made between the medial clusters in *dy'Mergher* and *de'Merher* are without foundation. As we have seen in Chapter 17, there is no documentary evidence for a spelling of the prefix as **dy*. There is also incidentally no documentary evidence for ‹eu› in the name for Tuesday; *Merth* would be more authentic. The attested forms of the prefix have *du, dew* and *de* only. The SWF should get rid of **dy* in these items and should also dispense with the apostrophe. Nothing has been omitted and the insertion of an apostrophe to indicate elision is unjustified.

INDEX

References are to paragraphs

INDEX

Lightning Source UK Ltd.
Milton Keynes UK
UKOW04f2352030118
315477UK00001B/136/P

9 781782 011859